Miami

Florida

HOTEL
COLLINS P

EVERYMAN
CITY GUIDES

EVERYMAN CITY GUIDES
Copyright © 2001 Everyman
Publishers Ltd, London

ISBN 1-84159-030-4

First published April 2001

Originally published in France by
Nouveaux Loisirs, a subsidiary of
Gallimard, Paris 2000, and in Italy
by Touring Editore, Srl., Milano
2000. Copyright © 2000
Nouveaux Loisirs,
Touring Editore, Srl.

SERIES EDITORS: Anne-Josyane
Magniant & Marisa Bassi
MIAMI EDITION:
COORDINATION
Ædelsa Atelier Tourisme
TCI : Asterisco srl, Milano
LAYOUT: Fiammetta Badalato
GRAPHICS: Yann Le Duc *assisted by*
Isabelle Dubois-Dumée
MINI-MAPS: Fiammetta Badalato and
Flavio Badalato
STREET MAPS: Touring Club Italiano

Translated by Yvonne Chapman
Edited and typeset by First
Edition Translations Ltd,
Cambridge, UK

Printed in Italy by
Editoriale Lloyd

Authors

Getting there and Further afield
Barbara Drake (1)
A graduate of the University of New York
and resident in Miami Beach, Barbara Drake
is a journalist and travel writer published in
The Village Voice, *Florida Heritage* and
Caribbean Lifestyles.

Where to stay and Where to shop
Elena De Siena (2)
Born in 1958, Elena De Siena is a journalist
with such magazines as *Moda*, *Vera* and *Taxi*.
She is a long-term resident of Miami,
where she is a correspondent of *La dolce
vita* magazine.

Where to eat
Victoria Pesce Elliott (3)
Victoria Pesce Elliott, a graduate of the
Columbia school of journalism, writes on
food and tourism for *New Times*, *South Florida
Gourmet* and *The Miami Herald*. She works
with the Macmillan publishing house, whose
guide to *Miami & The Keys* she has produced.

After dark
Carlos Eduardo Muñoz (4)
Carlos Eduardo Muñoz has always lived in
the thick of Miami's showbiz and nightlife.
As well as being a manager, producer, and
agent for acts, he also organizes theme
nights for major nightclubs.

What to see
Brian E. Rochlin (5)
Writer, editor and producer of cultural and
artistic events, Brian E. Rochlin is highly
knowledgeable about his city. He is a
regular reviewer for numerous publications,
including *Caribbean Travel & Life*.

Where to shop
Lorella Nerini Dal Pezzo (6)
This lawyer and journalist has lived in
Miami for 15 years, where she has run
companies specializing in production,
administration and marketing. She has also
contributed to various Italian magazines
and newspapers.

Things you need to know ➡ 6

Where to stay ➡ 16

Where to eat ➡ 38

After dark ➡ 64

What to see ➡ 78

Further afield ➡ 100

Where to shop ➡ 114

Maps ➡ 134

Symbols

- ☎ telephone
- ⇒ fax
- ● price or price range
- ◷ opening hours
- ▤ credit cards accepted
- ▤ credit cards not accepted
- ▼ toll-free number
- @ e-mail/website address
- ★ tips and recommendations

Access

- Ⓜ subway stations
- 🚌 bus (or tram)
- Ⓟ private parking
- 🅿 parking attendant
- 🚫 no facilities for the disabled
- ↘ train
- 🚗 car
- ⛵ boat

Hotels

- ☎ telephone in room
- ⫘ fax in room on request
- 🧊 minibar
- ▣ television in room
- ▥ air-conditioned rooms
- ◔ 24-hour room service
- ✗ caretaker
- ✗ babysitting
- ➕ meeting room(s)
- ⊘ no pets
- ☕ breakfast
- ☕ open for tea/coffee
- 🍴 restaurant
- ♫ live music
- ◉ disco
- ✦ garden, patio or terrace
- ✗ gym, fitness club
- ≋ swimming pool, sauna

Restaurants

- 🌱 vegetarian food
- 🏔 view
- 👔 formal dress required
- 🚬 smoking area
- 🍸 bar

Museums and galleries

- ▦ on-site store(s)
- ☞ guided tours
- 🍵 café

Stores

- ↔ branches, outlets

The Insider's Guide is made up of **8 sections** each indicated by a different color.

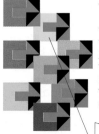

Things you need to know (mauve)
Where to stay (blue)
Where to eat (red)
After dark (pink)
What to see (green)
Further afield (oran[g])
Where to shop (yello[w])
Finding your way (purple)

🚌 Bus H,

Practical information is given for each particular establishment: opening times, prices, ways of paying, different services available.

"Bargain!"
This star marks good value hotels and restaurants.

How to use this guide

In the area
Where to stay: ➡ 18 ➡ 26
After dark: ➡ 68 ➡ 70 ➡ 7₄
What to see: ➡ 82 ➡ 86 ➡

The section
" In the area"
refers you (➡ 00) to
other establishments
that are covered in a
different section of the
guide but found in the
same area of the city.

South Beach/5th Street   B D

WASHINGTON
PARK

OCEAN BEACH
PARK

Washington

Street

Ocean

Collins

PIER
PARK

10
6

8

The small map
shows all the
establishments
mentioned and others
described elsewhere but
found "in the area", by
the color of the section.

**The name of the
district** is given above
the map. A grid
reference (**A** B-C 2)
enables you to find it in
the section on Maps at
the end of the book.

Not forgetting
■ Café Tabac (10) 136 Colli₁

The section "Not forgetting"
lists other useful addresses in the same area.

The opening page
to each section
contains an index
ordered alphabetically
(Getting there), by
subject or
by district (After dark)
as well as useful
addresses and advice.

**The section
"Things you need
to know"** covers
information on getting

to Miami and day-to-day
life in the city.

Theme pages
introduce a selection
of establishments on
a given topic.

**The "Maps"
section** of this guide
contains 6 street plans
of Miami followed by
a detailed index.

Electricity

Voltage: 110–120 volts. Plugs are different from British ones; you will need an adaptor to use your own electrical items. And if you buy electrical or electronic goods, ask for 'British' specifications.

Getting there

Average temperatures

December–April: 70–73°F

May–June: 77–86°F, humid

July–September: 82–104°F, maximum humidity

October–Novembe: 73–77°F.

Time difference

Florida is in the same time zone as New York. There is a five-hour time difference between the UK (GMT) and Florida: when it is 3pm in London, it is 10am in Miami.

Hurricanes

Between Aug. and Nov. Miami is prone to devastating hurricanes.

Insurance

Medical costs are very expensive, so for those coming from outside the US it is wise to take out adequate insurance before departure. Check with your insurer or tour operator that you are covered for repatriation on health grounds and loss of luggage.

57 Things
you need to Know

Public holidays

Martin Luther King Day:
3rd Monday in January
President's Day:
3rd Monday in February
Memorial Day:
last Monday in May
Independence Day:
July 4th
Labor Day:
1st Monday in September
Columbus Day: 2nd Monday in October
Veteran's Day: November 11th
Thanksgiving:
4th Thursday in November
Christmas: December 25th

Entry requirements

People from most European countries, including the United Kingdom, do not need a visa for stays of less than 90 days. You must have a valid passport, enough money to cover your expenses during your stay and a return air (or boat) ticket. No vaccinations are necessary, unless you are travelling from, or have recently visited, a country suffering from an epidemic.

INDEX

Basic facts

There are approximately 1,500 flights a day in and out of Miami. Miami International Airport (MIA) is served by 140 airlines and almost 35 million passengers pass through it each year, 15 million of them from abroad. Fort Lauderdale-Hollywood International Airport (FLHIA), which – despite its

Getting there

Directory

MIA (1)

4200 NW 21 St,
Miami, FL 33122

Information
☎ (305) 876-7000
@ www.miami-
airport.com

Police
☎ (305) 876-7373

Emergencies
☎ (305) 876-7070

Lost luggage
☎ (305) 876-7377

Customs
Non residents can import the following without paying duty: 1 liter of spirits, gifts with a value of less than $100 and 200 cigarettes (or 100 cigars, not Cuban). It is forbidden to import foodstuffs or plants, and sums of over $10,000 must be declared.

Airlines

Alitalia
☎ 800-223-5730

**American/
American Eagle**
☎ 800-433-7300

British Airways
Information and reservations::
☎ 305 347 6318
or 800 247 9297

Continental
☎ 800-525-0280

Delta
☎ 800-221-1212

TWA
☎ 800-221-2000

United
☎ 800-241-6522

Airport Connections- Miami

1) Buses
Buses leave from hall E (ground floor), but are not very frequent.

Bus 7
Downtown Miami
● $1.25
🕐 Mon.–Fri. 5.30am–9pm, Sat., Sun. 6.30am–7.30pm

Bus 37 South
Coral Gables and South Miami
🕐 6am–10pm

Bus 37 North
Hialeah
🕐 5.30am–11.30pm

Bus J South
Coral Gables
🕐 6am–0.30am

Bus J East
Miami Beach
🕐 4.30am–11.30pm

Bus 42
Coconut Grove

🕐 4.30am–11.30pm

2)Super Shuttle (2)
These shuttle buses carry passengers from MIA to their hotel, home or to the Port of Miami 24 hours a day.
● $9 to Downtown hotels; $14–18 to Miami Beach (between South Beach and Sunny Isles); $14 to Coconut Grove; $17 to Key Biscayne; $21 to FLHIA and Port Everglades. NB: the SuperShuttle does not pick up passengers at FLHIA.
☎ (305) 871-2000
@ www.supershuttle.com

3) Chauffeur-driven cars
Limousines from MIA or FLHIA must be reserved in advance.

A Touch of Class
☎ (305) 866-6664

Gold Coast
☎ (954) 776-7433

Vintage Rolls Royce Limousines
☎ (305) 444-7657

4) Taxis
Prices are calculated per journey, not per passenger. They include tolls and $1 airport tax.
● $17 to Coral Gables or Downtown; $18 to Miami Port; $30 to Key Biscayne; $24 to Miami Beach (between South Beach and 63rd Street); $41 to Golden Beach, Sunny Isles and Homestead.

5) Airport Region Taxi Service (ARTS)
These blue cars are for short journeys only: to the north as far as 36th Street, to the west to Palmetto Expressway (77th Ave), to the south to 7th Street and to the east to

name – also serves Miami is an important gateway for domestic flights.

Douglas Rd (37th Ave).
● *$7 inside the city; $10 outside.*

Car rental

Most car rental companies have branches at MIA and FLHIA (in the luggage collection area).

Avis
☎ 800-331-1212
Hertz
☎ 800-654-3131
Budget
☎ 800-527-0700
Dollar
☎ 800-800-4000
National
☎ 800-227-7368

Hotels

Miami International Airport Hotel
Hall E, upper level
☎ (305) 871-4100
or 800-327-1276
Wyndham Miami Airport
3900 NW 21st St.
☎ (305) 871-3800.

FLHIA (3)

Fort Lauderdale-Hollywood International Airport 1400 Lee Wagener Blvd, Fort Lauderdale, FL 33315

Information
☎ (954) 359-1200
Police
☎ (954) 359-1244
Assistance
☎ 911

Transport
1) Share Ride
Share Ride/Tri-County Airport Express Share Ride/Tri-County Airport Express offers shared rides to Miami-Dade County in Lincoln Towncars or shuttles.
● *$12 per person to MIA; $12 to Bal Harbour and Miami Beach; $20 to Coral Gables and Key Biscayne.*
2) Taxis
● *$48 to MIA; $26.50 to Bal*

Harbour; $65 to Key Biscayne.
3) Trains
Trains run every day from the airport to Miami. A free shuttle links FLHIA to the station.
☎ 800-874-7245
🕐 *5am–11pm*
● *$3 Mon.–Fri. $4 Sat., Sun.*

Airport hotels

Sheraton Fort Lauderdale Airport Hotel
1825 Griffin Rd, Dania, FL 33004
☎ (954) 920-3500
Fort Lauderdale Airport Hilton
1870 Griffin Rd, Dania, FL 33004
☎ (954) 920-3300

Connections MIA-FLHIA

Taxis
Prices are calculated per mile. ● *$48*

SuperShuttle and Share Ride
● *SuperShuttle (MIA-FLHIA), $21 Share Ride (FLHIA-MIA), $12*
Trains Tri-Rail (4)
● *Mon.–Fri. one way: $3; Sat., Sun. $4;*
🕐 *Weekdays approximately one train each hour. Weekends approximately one train every two and a half hours. Longer intervals in the afternoon.*
FLHIA-MIA:
🕐 *Mon.–Fri. 5.30am–9.13pm; Sat. 8.16am–10.31pm; Sun. 8.16am–9.01pm.*
MIA-FLHIA:
🕐 *Mon.–Fri. 5.28am–8.09pm, Sat. 9.16am–9.16pm, Sun. 9.16am–7.46pm.*

The age of tourism in Florida began in 1896 when Henry Flagler extended the Florida East Coast Railroad as far as Biscayne Bay. Trains and buses still offer regular, efficient services, but most visitors today arrive by air or by car. The port has 3 million visitors a year, making

Getting there

Trains

The national railroad company Amtrak provides connections between Miami and the east and west coasts. All trains make several stops. Travel times: New York–Miami: between 26 and 29 hours.
● *Return: $148–406 according to season and availability.*

Amtrak Information
☎ 800-USA-RAIL or 800-872-7245
Station (1)

8303 NW 37th Ave, Miami
☎ *(305) 835-1223*
🕐 *6.15am–10pm*

Car

Foreign driver's licenses are generally valid in the United States. But if your license is not in English, it would be advisable to get an International Driver License.

Getting there (2)
Interstate Highways
The I-95 goes down the east coast; the I-75

passes through Lake City and Tampa, then goes along the west coast; the I-10 serves the north of the state. The Florida Turnpike is a toll highway linking Orlando, West Palm Beach, Fort Lauderdale and Miami.

Highway Rules

Driving is on the right; road signs are quite easy to understand (direction signs are green, roads are indicated by their numbers).

Speed limits:
Most major roads:
55 mph
Most residential zones:
30 mph
Interstate Highways and Florida Turnpike:
55–70 mph

Road safety regulations

Seat belts must be worn. Babies and children must travel in child-seats fitted with restraints. Breaking the speed limit and drunken driving are dealt with severely by the

Miami the 'cruising capital of the world'.

2

police (tough fines, revocation of Driver's License or imprisonment).

Buses

Miami is also served by Greyhound buses. Journey times: New York–Miami, 28 hours.
● Round-trip $160

Greyhound (3)
Information
☎ 800-231-2222
4 branches in Miami.
Miami International Airport (4)
4111 NW 27th St

☎ (305) 871-1810
🕐 24 hours
North Miami Beach (5)
16560 NE 6th Ave
☎ (305) 945-0801
🕐 6am–11pm
Downtown Miami (6)
100 NW 6th St.
☎ (305) 374-6160
🕐 5am–11.30pm
South Miami
20505 S Dixie Hwy
☎ (305) 296-9072
🕐 8am–6pm

Boats

To enter the United States with your own boat (Atlantic

Coast, south of Sebastian Inlet), contact the United States Customs Office in Miami.
☎ 800-432-1216
If the boat weighs less than 5 tons, it may be possible to clear customs without having a physical inspection.
Haulover Marine Center (7)
15000 Collins Ave, Miami Beach
☎ (305) 945-3934
Miamarina (8)
401 Biscayne Blvd, Miami
☎ (305) 579-6955

Cruise ships

The **port of Miami** (9) is home to four major shipping companies and 20 cruise ships which link Miami to the Bahamas, the Caribbean, Mexico and Europe.
Port
1015 North American Way
Miami, FL 33131
☎ (305) 371-7678)

Main shipping lines
☎ (305) 599-2600
Cunard Line, Ltd.
☎ (305) 463-3000
Norwegian Cruise Lines
☎ (305) 436-4000
Royal Caribbean Cruise Lines
☎ (305) 539-6000

Basic facts

The city of Miami is fragmented, built partly on the mainland and partly on the many barrier islands that line the coast. Public transportation provides limited service, but is relatively slow; the car therefore remains the fastest and most practical way to get around Miami and all of Florida.

Getting there

Car

Signs (1)

Tourists would do well to stay on well-lighted roads in the hotel zones at night and to stay off the highways during rush hour (7–9am and 4–6pm).

Parking

Keep a supply of coins for parking meters. In Miami Beach you can also use $10 and $25 debit cards, which can be purchased from many hotels, markets and the Publix supermarket at 1920 West Ave, Miami Beach, 305-535-4268.

Public Transport

The Metro-Dade Transit Agency runs three different networks: Metrobus (70 different routes and 650 buses), Metrorail (21 miles of suburban trains) and Metromover (4 miles of aerial trains in the city center). Maps and timetables are free and may be ordered by mail. A ticket is valid for a single journey.

Government Center Station
111 NW 1st St.
Miami, FL 33128
☎ *(305) 654-6586*

Information on routes
☎ *(305) 770-3131*
🕔 *Mon.–Fri. 6am–10pm; Sat., Sun. 9am–5pm.*

Metrobus (2)

Metrobus stops are marked by blue and green signs bearing a bus logo and information about timetables and routes.
● *$1.25 (the driver does not give change and only takes coins); $0.60 reduced rate for students, senior citizens and the disabled; $1.50 Express route; concessions $0.75*
🕔 *4am–2.30am, depending on the route.*

Metrorail (3)

Metrorail goes from Downtown as far as Hialeah to the north and runs alongside Highway US 1 as far as Kendall to the south.
🕔 *5.30am–midnight (trains every 5–20 minutes)*
● *$1.25; concessions $ 0,60*

Metromover (4)

Two circular routes forming a loop in the Downtown area, with twenty-one stops, including the financial district of Brickell Ave and Bayside. Connects with Metrorail at the Government Center.
🕔 *Mon.–Fri. 5.30am–midnight; Sat., Sun. and public holidays 6am–midnight*

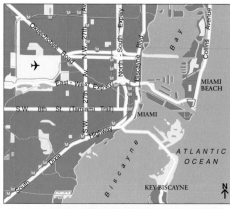

(trains every 2–3 minutes).
● *$0.25, concessions $0.10.*
Transfers
To change from one network to another, you need a transfer ticket: buy one on the bus for bus-to-bus or bus-to-train transfers, and at the station, before getting on the train, for train-to-bus transfers.
● *$0.25 for bus to bus and bus to train and vice versa (concessions $0.10); from train to train or train to bus $1 (concessions $0.50); free from bus or train to Metromover.*
Electrowave (5)
These electric

buses travel along Washington Ave linking South Beach to Lincoln Road Mall.
◐ *Mon.–Wed. 8am–2am; Thu.–Sat. 8am–4am; Sun. and public holidays 10am–2am.*
● *$0.25*

Taxis (6)
There are plenty of the traditional yellow cabs at the airports, large hotels and commercial centers.
● *$1.50 initial fare, then $2 per mile. Plus, a $1 surcharge for trips originating at the MIA.*
Central
☎ *(305) 532-5555*
Dispatch Service

☎ *(305) 888-4444*
Flamingo Taxi
☎ *(305) 759-8100*
Metro
☎ *(305) 888-8888*
Yellow
☎ *(305) 444-4444*

Roller Skates (7)
Roller-skates and roller-blades are one of the most popular ways of getting around South Beach. Several shops rent them out by the hour or the day.
Fritz's Skate Shop
726 Lincoln Road Mall, Miami Beach
☎ *(305) 532-1954*
● *$7.50 an hour; $22.50 a day; $14 from 6pm to midday; $50/200 deposit.*
Skate 2000
9525 S. Dixie Hwy, (Datran Dr)

☎ *(305) 665-6770*
Kendall ● $10/day rental including wrist, shin and knee guards. Children's sizes available.

Water taxi (8)
Though not very widely used, these boats carry up to 49 passengers and connect the mainland to the beaches. Departures from parks, hotels, restaurants, shopping centers etc.
Water Taxi
☎ *(954) 467-6677*
● *Biscayne Bay–Miami Beach $7 per person one way; $12 return per person.*

Basic facts

Because of the massive amount of immigration from South America and the Caribbean, Miami is essentially bilingual: as many people speak Spanish as speak English, and in some districts such as Little Havana, Spanish is the main language. The proximity of the Spanish and English speaking

Getting there

Money

Currency (1)
The monetary unit is the dollar ($), subdivided into 100 cents (¢). There are bills of 1, 5, 10, 20, 50 and 100 dollars and coins of 1 ('penny'), 5 ('nickel'), 10 ('dime'), 25 ('quarter') and 50 cents and also a relatively rare 1 dollar coin.

Banks
Banks are usually open from 9am to 4pm (Thu. 9am–7pm).

Traveler's Checks
Traveler's checks are accepted in many hotels, restaurants and shops. To exchange them, have your passport with you.

Exchange
International Currency Exchange

Miami International Airport, corridor
☎ (305) 876-0040
🕐 24 hours
USA Money Exchange (2)
1059 Collins Ave, Miami Beach
☎ (305) 673-6433
🕐 Mon.–Sat. 9.30am–6.50pm.

Credit cards
The most common form of payment in the United States; you will need a card to rent a car. Automatic cash machines can be found all over Miami.
If your card is lost or stolen
Visa
☎ 800-336-8472
American Express
☎ 800-992-3404
MasterCard
☎ 800-307-7309

The media

Local papers (3)
The Miami Herald, daily English paper; El Nuevo Herald, Spanish version of Miami Herald; Diario de las Americas, Spanish daily; The Miami New Times, free weekly in English, containing information on shows and restaurants.

Radio and TV
There are a large number of channels: for frequencies and program information see local press.

Internet
Web sites
Visit Florida
@ www.flausa.com
Great Miami Convention and Visitors Bureau
@www.miamiand beaches.com

Telephone (4)
For local calls, dial the area code 305 or 786, then the number. For elsewhere in the US, dial 1, then the local area code followed by the number.

Public telephones
● 35¢ for 3 minutes within the US.
Information
☎ 411
To call Miami from the UK dial 001 305, followed by the number.
To call the UK from Miami dial 001 44, followed by the number (without the 0).

Mail (5)
Post offices
Miami Beach (6)
1300 Washington Ave
☎ (305) 599-1787
Downtown Miami (7)
500 NW 2nd Ave
☎ (305) 639-4284
Coconut Grove (8)
3191 Grand Ave
☎ (305) 599-1750
Coral Gables (9)
251 Valencia Ave
☎ (305) 599-1795

communities has led to a hybrid slang: 'Do you speak Spanglish?'

☎ Mon.–Wed. 11am–6pm; Thu.–Sun. 11am–11pm: maps, leaflets, souvenirs, bicycle rental and guided walking tours of the Deco District.

Postal rates
● ordinary letter within the US, 33¢ postcard within the US, 20¢; ordinary letter to the UK, $1 (approx. 28g), 80¢ for each additional ounce; airmail letter to the UK, 60¢; airmail postcard to the UK, 55¢

Tourist offices
Greater Miami Convention & Visitors Bureau (10)
701 Brickell Ave, Suite 2700, Miami, FL 33131
☎ (305) 539-3000 or 800-933-8448
🕐 Mon.–Fri. 8.30am–5pm
Art Deco Welcome Center (11)
Miami Design Preservation League, Ocean Front Auditorium, 1001 Ocean Dr, Miami Beach, FL 33139

Emergencies
For the police, an ambulance or the fire service, call the toll free number
☎ 911 (available 24 hours).
Night-time emergencies
There are no doctors on call at night in the US. At night only the emergency units of hospitals are open. But expect a long wait! All Miami hospitals have fixed rates (except the Jackson Memorial Hospital, which charges according to income). Health costs are very high in the US and the patient is always responsible for paying the bill. You are therefore recommended to take out personal insurance before leaving home.

Emergency units open 24 hours
Mt. Sinai Medical Center
4300 Alton Rd, Miami Beach
☎ (305) 674-2200
Parkway Regional Hospital
160 NW 170th St., North Miami Beach
☎ (305) 651-1100
Jackson Memorial Hospital
1611 NW 12th Ave, Miami
☎ (305) 585-6901
Mercy Hospital
3663 S Miami Ave, Coconut Grove
☎ (305) 285-2171
Baptist Hospital of Miami
8900 N Kendall Dr, Miami
☎ (305) 596-6556
South Miami Hospital
6200 SW 73rd St., South Miami
☎ (305) 662-8181

Pharmacies open 24 hours
There is a pharmacist permanently on duty in several

Walgreen Drugstores.
1845 Alton Rd South Beach
☎ (305) 531-8868
5731 SW Bird Rd Miami
☎ (305) 666-0757
791 NE 167 St., North Miami Beach
☎ (305) 652-7332
7910 NW 27th Ave, Miami
☎ (305) 691-0881

Lost property
Dade County Police Lost & Found
☎ (305) 375-3366

UK Consulate
1001 S Bayshore Dr
☎ (305) 374-1522

Australian Consulate
Suite 208, 2525 SW Third Avenue
☎ (305) 858-7633
➦ (305) 857-0044

Canadian Consulate
200 South Biscagne Boulevard Suite 1600
☎ (305) 579-1600
➦ (305) 374-6674

"Boutique hotel"
This describes many of the small Art-Deco buildings on Miami Beach,
but it can also refer to delightful hotels found in other districts.

Where to stay

High and low seasons

High season is from December to March, low season from April to November, when hotel prices can fall by 50%.

Tips

Anyone offering you a service will expect a tip. There is an unwritten code of tariffs for each occasion:

Airport porter
$1–3 per item of luggage
Taxi driver
10–15% of the fare plus $1 per item of luggage
Bell boy
$0.5–2 per item of luggage
Hotel doorman
$1 for calling a taxi
Chambermaid
$1–2 per person per night
Shoeshine
$1–2
Parking attendant
$1–3 per vehicle
Waiter
15–20% of the bill
Barman
10–15% of the bill
Hairdresser/barber
15–20% of the cost.

Prices

Hotels listed here are grouped in five price ranges, based on the price of a double room in the high season. Hotel tax and breakfast are included.

49
Hotels

THE INSIDER'S FAVORITES

Hotels ring the changes

A spate of building and renovating will result in many more choices for the money-is-no-object set come 2001. The Mandarin Oriental in downtown, The Four Seasons in Brickell Key, a W Hotel and The Shore Club on Miami beach, plus three Ritz-Carltons are just some of the big players coming to town.

Where to stay

Century Hotel (1)
140 Ocean Dr, Miami Beach, FL 33139
☎ (305) 674-8855 ➡ (305) 538-5733

🖼 Bus W, H; Electrowave 🅿 **27 rooms** (and 4 suites) ●●● 📺 🔲 🔳 🗃 🎞 safe 📶 🔲 📺 ⬛ ➕ 📼 1-888-982-3688 @ www.centuryhotelsobe.com

An elegant and welcoming hotel built by Henry Hohauser in 1939 the Century is a work of art. As soon as you enter the ingeniously lit entrance hall, with its many paintings and sculptures by the artist Wilhem Moser, you are struck by its lavish eclecticism. The simple lines of the furniture in the rooms help to create a sleek and cosmopolitan atmosphere. While cushy white towels and cool gray marble in the bathrooms create a sense of freshness.

The Hotel (2)
801 Collins Ave, Miami Beach, FL 33139
☎ (305) 531-5796 ➡ (305) 531-3222

🖼 Bus C, H, K, M, W; Electrowave 🅿 🛎 **48 rooms** (and 4 suites, 1 penthouse) ●●●● 📺 🔲 🕐 7am–11pm 🔳 🗃 📶 III safe 📶 Wish 📺 🔲 ⬛ ⬛ 🎿 🕸 🕸 🎴 ⬛ 🍴 📼 1-877-THE-HOTEL @ www.thehotelofsouthbeach.com

Who could imagine that the simple white façade with a Tiffany sign would hide such an explosion of colors and shapes inside? This hidden exuberance is the work of Todd Oldham who redesigned the interior of this Art-Deco hotel in 1998. Everything in it, from the large mosaic in the hall to the hundred glass lanterns suspended from the ceiling of the restaurant, is unusual. The *pièce de résistance* is the terrace swimming pool decorated to give the impression of the sea meeting the sky.

Pelican Hotel (3)
826 Ocean Dr, Miami Beach, FL 33139
☎ (305) 673-3373 ➡ (305) 673-3255

🖼 Bus C, H, K, M, W; Electrowave 🛎 **22 rooms** (and 3 suites, 1 penthouse) ●●● 📺 🔲 🕐 🔳 🗃 ⬛ III safe 📶 Pelican Café 📺 🔲 ⬛ 🕸 📼 1-800-7PELICAN @ www.pelicanhotel.com

In this area frequented by the world of fashion and show business, each room has its own name and is decorated and furnished accordingly. The most extraordinary is the James Bond Penthouse, with its round bed, Pop-Art posters, mosaic bathroom and huge aquarium.

Not forgetting

■ **The Park Central (4)** 640 Ocean Dr, Miami Beach, FL 33139 ☎ (305) 538-1611 ➡ (305) 534-7520 ●●● *Affiliated to the Historic Hotels of America, and built in 1937 by Henry Hohauser, 'The blue gem' has housed the likes of Clark Gable and Rita Hayworth among its guests; with its Art-Deco furniture it retains an air of times past.*
■ **The Wave Hotel (5)** 350 Ocean Dr, Miami Beach, FL 33139 ☎ (305) 673-0401 ➡ (305) 531-9385 ●●● *Saporiti furniture is decked out in shades of blue and white.*
■ **Whitelaw Hotel (6)** 808 Collins Ave, Miami Beach, FL 33139 ☎ 1-888-554-3123 ➡ (305) 398-7010 ●●● *This new establishment, inspired by the most famous (and most expensive) hotels, has dared to use white for everything.*

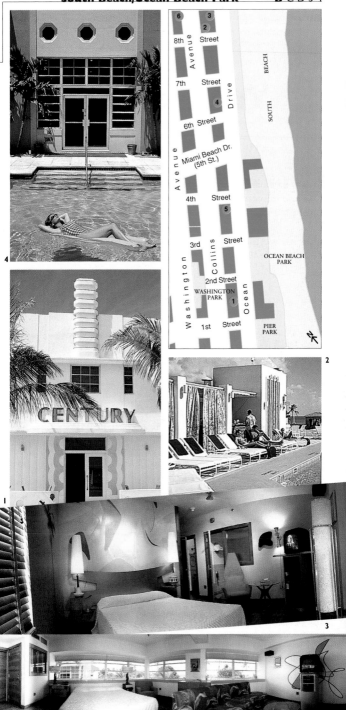

In the area
 Where to eat: ➡ 44
After dark: ➡ 66 ➡ 68 ➡ 70 ➡ 74
What to see: ➡ 82 ➡ 86 ➡ 98
Where to shop: ➡ 116

Where to stay

Hotel Leon (7)
841 Collins Ave, Miami Beach, FL 33139
☎ (305) 673-3767 ➡ (305) 673-5866

🚌 Bus C, H, K, M, W; Electrowave 🛏 *12 rooms (and 5 suites, 1 penthouse)* ●●●
🕯 extra ▬ ▣ ☎ ▥ safe ▣ ▥ 🛅 🗙 🖭 www.hotelleon.com

This delightful hotel hidden among palm trees sought its inspiration from
the countries around the Mediterranean. The spacious rooms have light-
colored wood floors; the drapes around the beds and the chair covers
are made from white cotton. The bathrooms are in terracotta, the bath is
tucked away in an alcove, and the sinks are stainless steel. The penthouse
is a dream: a huge room with exposed beams and an adjoining wooden
deck leads to an oversized sandbox dotted with parasols and small
tables. There is however a price to pay: the stairs are steep.

The Mermaid Guest House (8)
909 Collins Ave, Miami Beach, FL 33139
☎ (305) 538-5324 ➡ (305) 538-2822

🚌 Bus C, H, K, M, W; Electrowave 🛏 *9 rooms (and 1 suite)* ●● ▣ *only in some
rooms* ☎ 🛅 ▥ ▥ 🎵 🎿 🗙

A small and casual guesthouse nestled in a tropical garden, which exudes
the ambience of the Caribbean. The beds--draped in mosquito nets--have
batik covers and the bathrooms, like the rooms themselves, are vibrantly
colored.

Hotel Astor (9)
956 Washington Ave, Miami Beach, FL 33139
☎ (305) 531-8081 ➡ (305) 531-3193

🚌 Bus C, H, K, M, W; Electrowave *17 rooms (and 22 suites, 1 penthouse)* ●●●
🕯 ▬ 🕐 7.30am–11pm ▣ ☎ 🛅 ▥ safe 🍴 Astor Place ▥ ▣ ▥ 🛅 🚭
🗙 ▥ 1-800-270-4981 @ www.hotelastor.com

This magnificent lobby is by Handerson (1936). This understated and
elegant hotel was thoroughly refurbished in 1995. It has since become
one of the hottest spots for those in the know. Popular for its relatively
reasonable prices and also because of its stunning bar, famous restaurant,
comfy rooms, large marble bathrooms, and unparalleled service. The
compact pool is fed by a dramatic waterfall.

Not forgetting
■ **The Kent (10)** 1131 Collins Ave, Miami Beach, FL 33139 ☎ (305) 604-
5068 ➡ (305) 531-0720 ●● *Low tables, mahogany and bamboo chairs, batik-
covered armchairs and footstools, wooden chaise longues in greens and blues,
embossed metal lamps: the foyer furnishings are a happy mixture of Africa and
Asia brightening up the 1930s architecture. The rooms have only contemporary
furniture, some in natural wood for a minimalist style.* ■ **Hotel Nash (11)**
1120 Collins Ave, Miami Beach, FL 33139 ☎ (305) 674-7800 ➡ (305) 538-8288
●●● *A brand new hotel with sinuous styling, a world-class restaurant and three
compact swimming pools. Comfortable rooms enlivened by unusual pieces of
furniture.* ■ **Essex House Hotel and Suites (12)** 1001 Collins Ave,
Miami Beach, FL 33139 ☎ (305) 534-2700 ➡ (305) 532-3827 ●●● *Venetian
tiling in the large lobby, piano and a mural of the Everglades by Earl Lepan over the
fireplace. Fabrics in a beautiful shade of red in the spacious rooms.*

In the heart of the Art-Deco district beyond Ocean Drive you can find up-to-date establishments with Mediterranean and Oriental influences.

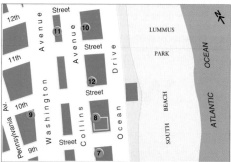

7

9

10

11

8

8

➡ Where to stay

The Tides (13)
1220 Ocean Dr, Miami Beach, FL 33139
☎ (305) 604-5070 ➠ (305) 604-5180

🔲 Bus C, H, K, W; Electrowave 🅿 🔳 **42 suites** (and 3 penthouses) ●●●●● 🔳 $ 10 🔲 🔳 📶 🔳 🔳 safe 🔳 1220, The Terrace Restaurant 🎵 🔳 🔳 🔳 🔳 🔳 🔳 🔳 🔳 🔳 🔳 🔳 🔳 🔳 1-800-OUTPOST @ www.islandoutpost.com

The elegance and style of this Art-Deco hotel surpass all the others on Ocean Drive. The view is in keeping with the majestic building, which is the tallest on Ocean Drive: all the suites have ocean views and come with their own telescopes. Since its refurbishment in 1977, The Tides has shone like a beacon over the high seas.

Hotel Ocean (14)
1230-1238 Ocean Dr, Miami Beach, FL 33139
☎ (305) 672-2579 ➠ (305) 672-7665

🔲 Bus C, H, K, W; Electrowave 🅿 🔳 **13 rooms** (and 12 suites, 1 penthouse) ●●● 🔳 🔳 🔳 7.30am–midnight 🔳 🔳 🔳 🔳 safe 🔳 Les Deux Fontaines 🎵 🔳 🔳 🔳 🔳 🔳 🔳 🔳 🔳 1-800-783-1725 @ www.hotelocean.com

This is the place for those who prefer something more cozy than the somewhat stark Art-Deco style. The small fireplaces, old-fashioned furniture, floral armchairs and linen curtains and bedcovers make you feel you are in an old French country house.

Cavalier (15)
1320 Ocean Dr, Miami Beach, FL 33139.
☎ 305/604-5000 ➠ 305/531-5543

🔲 MDTA C, H, K, W; Electrowave 🅿 🔳 $14 🅿 $6 **45 rooms** ●●● 🔳 🔳 🔳 🔳 Winter $185–$210 double; $275–$350 suite. Off-season $95–$155 double; $230–$285 suite. Additional person $15 extra. AE, DC, DISC, MC, V.🔳 no pets 🔳 1-800-OUTPOST 🔳 24-hour service @ www.islandoutpost.com

A relatively inexpensive option on Ocean Drive, the Cavalier is a modest choice in an ideal location. Funky prints cover the walls, which are the colors of a Caribbean sunrise. Palm trees brush the ceilings of the handsome deco lobby, where young trendy guests make their way to their rooms. As in all other Outpost hotels, rooms come equipped with CD players and lots of good music.

Not forgetting

■ **Cardozo (16)** 1300 Ocean Dr, Miami Beach, FL 33139 ☎ (305) 535-6500 ➠ (305) 532-3563 ●●● *Henry Hohauser had the original idea for this very beautiful building with curved lines in 1939; it was undergoing a major renovation in late 2000 by owner, Cuban pop star, Gloria Estefan and husband Emilio.* ■ **The Winter Haven (17)** Winter Haven South Beach 1400 Ocean Drive, Miami Beach, FL 33139 ☎ 305-531-5571 or 800-395-2322 ➠ 305-538-6387 ●●● *Reopened in mid 2000 after extensive renovation, this six-story gem has spacious, comfortable rooms* ■ **Clay Hotel & International Hostel (18)** 1438 Washington Ave, Miami Beach, FL 33139 ☎ (305) 534-2988 ➠ (305) 673-0346 ● *Occupies a whole block in the most historic district of Miami; its façade, on Española Way, is a masterpiece. Spacious, with all the essential services, it is without doubt the best kept hostel in the US, and the one with the most character.*

The 'Tropical' variety of Art-Deco architecture is seen at its best in the part of Ocean Drive south of Española Way: The Tides, Leslie, Cardozo, and Cavalier are the finest examples.

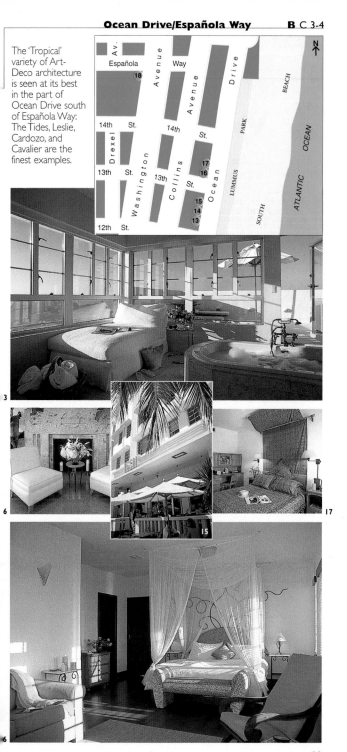

Where to stay

The National Hotel (19)
1667 Collins Ave, Miami Beach, FL 33139
☎ (305) 532-2311 ➡ (305) 534-1426

🚌 Bus C, H, K; Electrowave 🅿 🏊 *142 rooms* (and 5 suites) ●●●● 🌿 extra ▱
🕕 6am–midnight ▱ 📞 📶 🍴 safe 🍽 Café Mosaic ▾ Deco Lounge 🎵 🎵 Fri.
▮ 🎿 ♿ ➕ 🏋 🌊 🎾 ★ 🌙 📺 1-800-327-8370 @ www.nationalhotel.com

One of the most luxurious hotels of the 1940s has been restored in
keeping with the Art-Deco style. A beautiful tropical garden borders the
longest swimming pool in Florida. Pure nostalgia. By next season, the
National will have been bought by the fabulously popular Delano Hotel
next door. It can only get better.

Delano (20)
1685 Collins Ave, Miami Beach, FL 33139
☎ (305) 672-2000 ➡ (305) 5320099

🚌 Bus C, H, K; Electrowave 🅿 🏊 *208 rooms* (and 20 suites) ●●●●● 🌿 extra
▱ 🕕 📞 📶 🍴 safe 🍽 Blue Door ▾ ▮ 🎿 🎿 🎾 ♿ ➕ 🏋 🌊 🎾 🌐 ★
🌙 📺 1-800-555-5001

This Philippe Starck creation is the trendiest hotel in Miami. With its
sweeping white curtains, mammoth columns and gleaming parquet
floors, the huge foyer is only an appetizer. Beyond this is an Alice-in-
Wonderland spirit to the decor: in the garden a giant chess-board stands
next to a small wrought iron bed, and the swimming pool contains a
silver table with chairs, which seems to float in the shallow end. One
wall of the restaurant is covered with African masks. Everything in the
bungalows and rooms is white: bed, floor, walls, linens and the trays
serving as shelves in the bathroom. The atmosphere of Greece is
created on the terrace with the blue and white colors and hanging
flower vases and in the spa, which is open only to women during the day

The Albion Hotel (21)
1650 James Ave, Miami Beach, FL 33139
☎ (305) 913-1000 ➡ (305) 674-0507

🚌 Bus C, H, K; Electrowave 🅿 🏊 *87 rooms* (and 9 suites) ●●●● 🌿 extra
▱ 🕕 📞 📶 📶 🍴 The Pantry ▾ ▮ 🎿 🎾 ♿ ➕ 🏋 🌊 🎾 ★
📺 1-800-RUBELLS @ www.rubellhotels.com 🔑 **Greenview Hotel** Washington
Ave, Miami Beach, FL 33139 ☎ (305) 531-6588 ➡ (305) 531-4580

This hotel, designed by Igor Polevitsky (1939), the inventor of nautical
Art Deco, gives you the impression of being on an ocean liner with its
port-holes, waterfall wall and metal railings. Refurbished in 1997 by the
Rubell family, it offers airy rooms decorated by the avant-garde architect
Carlos Zapata in harmonious gray and white.

Not forgetting

■ **Loews (22)** 1601 Collins Ave, Miami Beach, FL 33139 ☎ (305) 604-1601
➡ (305) 604-3999 ●●●● *Opened in 1997, this opulent hotel is the first to be
built on Miami Beach in nearly 40 years. Provides all the comfort and services its
splendor demands.*
■ **The Raleigh (23)** 1775 Collins Ave, Miami Beach, FL 33139
☎ (305) 534-6300 ➡ (305) 538-8140 ●●●● *Comfortable. Furnishings
date from the fifties.*

A selection of establishments for those who still like to feel at home while on holiday. They provide the quality, comfort and service of a large hotel, with the advantages of a private apartment: a kitchenette, allowing you to avoid stuffy hotel restaurants some evenings, a living room for relaxing after a day at the beach or shopping...

Where to stay

The Bentley Luxury Suite Hotel (24)
510 Ocean Dr, Miami Beach, FL 33139
☎ (305) 538-1700 ➠ (305) 532-4865

🖪 Bus C, H, K, M, W; *Electrowave* 🅿 🈲 *53 suites* ●●●● ▱ ▣ 🖻 🛗 ⊞ *safe*
🦽 🧖 🏊 ★ 🚼 🔌 📺 *1-877-236-8510* @ *www.thebentley.com*

With an Italian sense of design and an American sense of practicality, the Bentley scores high on all counts. Antique furniture, old clocks, divans draped in white cotton and high beds. These suites are so like private apartments, they make it easy for the traveler to forget he is in a hotel. The light carpets and honey-colored walls give an airy feel. The bathrooms are luxurious and spacious. Other plus points include courteous staff, and an attractive terrace where you can sunbathe, have a swim or admire the view from a Jacuzzi.

Casa Grande Suite Hotel (25)
834 Ocean Dr, Miami Beach, FL 33139
☎ (305) 672-7003 ➠ (305) 673-3669

🖪 Bus C, H, K, M, W; *Electrowave* 🈲 *34 suites* ●●●● ▱ 🕐 *7am–11pm* ▣ 🖻
🛗 ⊞ *safe* 🍴 🦽 🍽 🔆 🧖 🔌 📺 *1-800-OUTPOST* @ *www.islandoutpost.com*

As you enter the foyer, the pillars from Rajasthan and Balinese furniture convey the atmosphere of the Orient. All the details help to create a fairy-tale universe – in the image of the peaceful Buddhas sitting enthroned between the *bas reliefs* and richly decorated mirrors, Indian carpets and precious materials. Mahogany four-poster beds and blue-green mosaics in the bathrooms: every feature contributes to the sublime decor.

Marlin (26)
1200 Collins Ave, Miami Beach, FL 33139
☎ (305) 604-5063 ➠ (305) 673-9609

🖪 Bus C, H, K, M, W; *Electrowave* 🅿 🈲 *13 suites* ●●●● 🎬 *extra* ▱ 🕐 ▣
🖻 🛗 ⊞ *safe* 🍸 🦽 🍽 🔆 📺 *1-800-OUTPOST* @ *www.islandoutpost.com*

The rounded shapes of this hotel were designed by L. Murray Dixon in 1939. The bright purple exterior makes it stand out from the others of its ilk. It seems to appeal to the eclectic clientele, many who come from the worlds of music, fashion and show biz. It has silver curtains and walls, metal pillars and Surrealist armchairs. The scene is set as soon as you enter the foyer. The Marlin Bar is in the Techno style; the Cyber Lounge tends toward industrial-eclectic; the Shabeen Lounge has brightly colored furniture and subdued lighting conveying a feel of the Caribbean. Extravagance is the order of the day. All the suites come with full stainless steel kitchens, Webtv, martini bars and a large selection of international CDs.

Not forgetting

■ **Sunterra Resort at the Savoy (27)** 425-455 Ocean Dr, Miami Beach, FL 33139 ☎ (305) 532-0200 ➠ (305) 534-7436 ●●●● *Every apartment here is unique. Rooms come in Art-Nouveau style or with gilded motifs.* ■ **The Four Ambassadors (28)** 801 S Bayshore Dr, Miami, FL 33131 ☎ (305) 371-6500 ➠ (305) 789-2900 ●●● *In a hidden corner of downtown, this suite hotel promises tranquillity and magnificent views over the bay.*

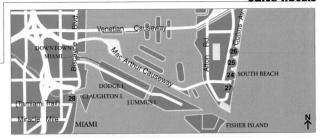

27

27

24

25

26

In the area
 Where to eat: ➡ 60
➡ After dark: ➡ 74
➡ What to see: ➡ 98
➡ Where to shop: ➡ 120

Where to stay

Sheraton Bal Harbour Resort (29)
9701 Collins Ave, Bal Harbour, FL 33154
☎ (305) 865-7511 ➡ (305) 864-2601

Bus H, K, S, T P 632 rooms (and 6 suites, 4 small villas) ●●●● extra safe Al Carbon Steakhouse 1-800-999-9898 @ www.starwoods.com

This establishment, whose guests have included Bill Gates and Bill and Hillary Clinton, was awarded the "Four Diamond Award" in 1999. A wood and rope bridge, the "mystic bridge", suspended over the lagoon, leads to the swimming pools, an aquatic fantasy which was used for outside scenes in "Analyze This" with de Niro. Waterfalls, toboggans, Jacuzzi and children's pools. It all cost a mere 12 million dollars, but it keeps you amused when you get bored with the beach.

Beach House Bal Harbour (30)
9449 Collins Ave, Bal Harbour, FL 33154
☎ (305) 535-8600 ➡ (305)-535-8601

Bus H, K, S, T P 150 rooms (and 15 suites) ●●● extra safe The Atlantic Restaurant banqueting room 1-877-RUBELLS @ www.rubellhotels.com

This Ralph Lauren-designed newcomer has the feel of a luxurious private house, decorated in white and Dresden blue, taking its inspiration from casual Nantucket beach houses. As soon as you walk in, the colors, the flowers and the cotton-covered furniture create a welcoming and fresh atmosphere. The plant-filled Bamboo Room full of Asiatic statues invites you to relax here, as do the large wicker-filled guest rooms. With a gorgeous seaside vista and a fantastic lobby restaurant, this is the place for hip and tasteful visitors from all over the world. The seahorse bar is a fun place to meet for a drink.

Dezerland Surfside Beach Hotel (31)
8701 Collins Ave, Miami Beach, FL 33141
☎ (305) 865-6661 ➡ (305) 866-2630

Bus H, K, S, T 240 rooms ●● extra 1-800-331-9346 @ www.dezerhotels.com

You could think you were in an episode of 'Happy Days' ... or in a drive-in. Posters of Elvis Presley, Marilyn Monroe, James Dean; records, signs, gas pumps. And to cap it all, those famous 1950s American cars parked in the foyer and in the restaurant. They were collected by the eccentric billionaire Michael Dezer. There is nothing to stop you having a snack perched on a pink Cadillac. The bathrooms could be considered a bit on the small side, but the recently refurbished rooms are a decent size and many have a grand view of the sea. Young people and sporty types should appreciate the water sports center, which offers jet-skis, surfing and parasailing.

Not forgetting
■ **The Sea View Hotel on the Ocean (32)** 9909 Collins Avenue, Bal Harbour, FL 33154 ☎ (305) 866-4441 ➡ (305) 866-1898 or 800 447 1010 ●●● America as it was. Its charm attracts visitors from the world of politics.

Signposts are unnecessary to mark the way in to Bal Harbour, an elegant enclave on Collins Avenue between Surfside and Haulover Park; look for perfectly manicured palm trees and shrubs, well-coifed couples in blazers and loafers, luxurious hotels, pricey boutiques and chauffeur-driven limousines.

29

30

30

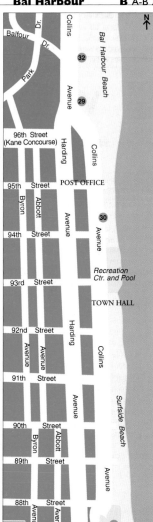

31

In the area
 Where to eat: ➡ 50
 After dark: ➡ 72 ➡ 76
 What to see: ➡ 88
 Where to shop: ➡ 126 ➡ 130

Where to stay

Hotel Inter-Continental Miami (33)
100 Chopin Plaza, Miami, FL 33131
☎ (305) 577-1000 ➡ (305) 577-0384

Ⓜ *Metrorail Government Center; Metromover Bayfront Park* Ⓟ ⛄ *609 rooms (and 30 suites)* ●●● Ⓥ *extra* ▣ ◐ ▣ ◙ Ⅲ▮▮ Ⅲ *safe* 🍴 *Indigo Restaurant* 🎵 ▮▮
@ www.interconti.com   📞 1-800-327-3005

In the heart of the financial and business district, this hotel is an ideal base for business people, offering excellent service in impeccable surroundings. A huge Henry Moore sculpture, The Spindle, greets guests in the lobby: 70 tons of marble topped by a pyramid-shaped glass and steel lamp. The rooms and marble bathrooms offer every comfort. Some overlook the bay, others the city. In their free time, guests can enjoy the swimming pool, and a gymnasium on the 5th floor or travel a few blocks to the nearby Bayside market place.

Hyatt Regency Miami (34)
Miami Convention Center, 400 SE 2nd Ave, Miami, FL 33131
☎ (305) 358-1234 ➡ (305) 358-0529

Ⓜ *Metrorail Government Center; Metromover Knight Center* Ⓟ ⛄ *561 rooms (and 51 suites)* ●●●● Ⓥ *extra* ▣ ◐ ▣ ◙ Ⅲ Ⅲ *safe* 🍴 *Riverwalk* 🎵 🎵 ▮▮
📞 1-800-233-1234 @ www.hyatt.com

Twenty-seven meeting rooms, one conference room capable of holding up to 5,000 people and a business center make this hotel situated near the Miami Convention Center and the University of Miami an ideal location for groups and conferences. But care has also been taken to ensure clients can relax in a comfortable, pleasant atmosphere. A fountain, a piano and a contemporary work of art add to the charm of the Art-Deco lobby. The recently refurbished rooms and suites offer very pleasant views over the river or the city.

Sheraton Biscayne Bay Hotel (35)
495 Brickell Ave, Miami, FL 33131 ☎ (305) 373-6000 ➡ (305) 374-6619

Ⓜ *Metrorail Government Center; Metromover Brickell Loop, 5th St.* 🚌 *Bus 24-West* Ⓟ ⛄ *594 rooms (and 14 suites)* ●●● Ⓥ *À la carte* ▣ ◐ *6.30am–11pm* ▣ ◉ Ⅲ 🍴 *Regatta Bar & Grill* ▮▮ 🎵 *banqueting room*
📞 1-800-325-3535 @ www.sheraton.com

This functional and elegant hotel, only a short distance from the financial district Downtown, occupies a superb location. The rooms reflect the tropical ambience, extravagance and taste for color peculiar to Florida, and enjoy exceptional vistas over the bay, the parks or the recent archeological excavations in the neighborhood, which revealed a sacred Indian stone circle.

Not forgetting
■ **Everglades Hotel (36)** 244 Biscayne Blvd, Miami, FL 33132
☎ (305) 379-5461 ➡ (305) 577-8390 ●● *A stone's throw from Bayside. For those needing a good central location at a reasonable price.*

Downtown experienced a decline in the 1950s, but it is gradually re-discovering its role at the hub of city life: bars, restaurants, elegant boutiques ... and acrobats perform on the streets of the financial district of Miami, which used to be rather dull.

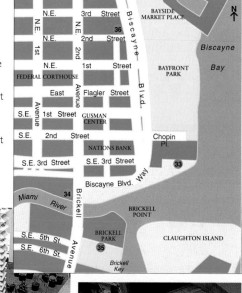

34

33

35

Refined atmospheres, interiors worthy of a Thousand and One Nights, impeccable service ... not to mention spas, golf courses, swimming pools and private beaches... Miami's luxury hotels attend to your every whim, so, just like Aladdin, you can have whatever you want. Whether your desire is for a ride in a limousine, to fish in the open sea, to fly over the

Where to stay

38

37

The Fisher Island Club (37)
I Fisher Island Dr, Fisher Island, FL 33109
☎ (305) 535-6020 ➡ (305) 535-6026

🚌 Bus C-Beach, S-Aventura, K-Haulover + Ferry 🏨 *60 accommodation units* *(rooms, apartments, villas)* ●●●●● 🍽 *À la carte* ⬛ ⏰ *6am–midnight* ⬛ 📷 🛗 🎛 *safe* 🍴 📺 🖥 *The Garwood Lounge* 🎵 📺 🖥 ♿ 🎰 ➕ *banqueting room* 🏊 〰 🎾 🎱 ✳ 🌙 📺 *1-800-537-3708* @ *www.fisherisland-florida.com*

Disembarking on Fisher Island involves lots of checks – it is like landing at a fortress. This island is inhabited by billionaires and has two sailing harbors, a helicopter landing pad, a golf course and a spa. Accommodation is dotted around tropical gardens with pink flamingos and beaches of white sand imported from the Bahamas. A house that was once the residence of the Vanderbilts (1925) is today one of the most exclusive hotels in the world; the old outbuildings contain the suites, furnished with antiques; in the main residence are the restaurants and lounges where you can relax by the fire listening to classical music.

Turnberry Isle Resort and Club (38)
19999 W Country Club Dr, Aventura, FL 33180
☎ (305) 936-2929 ➡ (305) 933-6560

🚌 Bus 3-Diplomat 🏨 *354 rooms (and 41 suites)* ●●●●● 🍽 *extra* ⬛ ⏰ ⬛ 📷 🛗 🛗 🎛 *safe* 🍴 *Veranda Restaurant & Bar* 🎵 📺 🖥 ♿ 🎰 ➕ *banqueting room* 🏊 〰 🎾 🎱 ✳ 🌙 📺 *1-800-327-7028* @ *www.turnberryisle.com*

The complex consists of a tropical garden and a park, golf courses and tennis courts where champions often play, a spa, a private beach and a sailing harbor. The surroundings feel European, like a sort of English club

city in a helicopter... Just make your wish and pay the price!

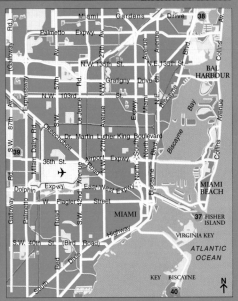

with Mediterranean architecture. Oriental carpets, terracotta and wood in the rooms, marble and a Jacuzzi in the bathrooms... The restaurant is open only to hotel guests or club members and serves excellent food.

Doral Golf Resort and Spa (39)
4400 NW 87th Ave, Miami, FL 33178 ☎ (305) 592-2000 ➠ (305) 594-4682

🚌 Bus 36-Cogar, 87 🅿 🛎 **646 rooms** (and 48 suites) ●●●● 🛎 À la carte 🔲 ⏰ 6.30am–midnight 🔲 ☎ 🛏 ⫴ safe 🍴 The Atrium 🎵 🔲 🍽 ♿ ✗ ✚ 📺 🏊 ✗ 🎾 ✸ 🎿 ✅ 1-800-71DORAL @ www.doralgolf.com

The clientele is mostly top sports people, attracted by the international tournaments organized on its famous golf courses. Some families have started to come since the opening of the Blue Lagoon, a complex of swimming pools with water slides, bridges and waterfalls, and small beaches dotted with umbrellas. The large rooms have a terrace or a patio, which opens on to the green. The health club offers all the best treatments, including some based on mud or mineral salts ... and very competent professionals provide a personalized follow-up.

Not forgetting

■ **Sonesta Beach Resort Key Biscayne (40)** 350 Ocean Dr, Key Biscayne, FL 33149 ☎ (305) 361-2021 ➠ (305) 361-2082 ●●●●● *This hotel offers a wide range of activities and is always attentive to your needs.*

In the area
 Where to eat: ➡ 56 ➡ 58
 After dark: ➡ 72
 After dark: ➡ 96
 Where to shop: ➡ 128

Where to stay

The Biltmore Hotel (41)
1200 Anastasia Ave, Coral Gables, FL 33134
☎ **(305) 445-1926** ➡ **(305) 913-3159**

🚌 Bus 72 🍴 *252 rooms* (and 28 suites) ●●●● 📺 *extra* ▢ ⏲ ▣ 🖥 Ⅲ 🛏
Ⅲ *safe* 🍴 *La Palme d'Or, Courtyard Café* 🔊 🎵 ▣ 🎭 ♿ 🔋 ✕ ➕ 🈲
✕ ⊞ ★ 🌙 📺 *1-800-727-1926* @ www.biltmorehotel.com

Miami's oldest hotel and a city landmark, the Biltmore was built in 1926
and was granted national recognition as an official National Historical
Landmark in 1996 – one of only two operating hotels in Florida to
receive the designation. Always a popular destination for golfers,
including many politicians and celebrities, the Biltmore is situated on a
lush rolling 18-hole course that is as challenging as it is beautiful.
Surrounding the property are tropical plants and statues as well as the
largest hotel swimming pool in the country. It is a wonderful option for
those seeking a luxurious getaway in a self-contained, quiet setting that is
still convenient to the shops, the airport and beaches. Rooms are
decorated with period reproductions and light, tropical prints. And while
ghost stories are recounted around the fireplace, most agree that this is
a place for those who appreciate living well.

Omni Colonnade Hotel (42)
180 Aragon Avenue, Coral Gables, FL 33134
☎ **(305) 441-2600** ➡ **(305) 445-3929**

🚌 Bus 24, 37 🍴 *137 rooms* (and 20 suites) ●●●● 📺 *extra* ▢ ⏲ ▣ 🖥 Ⅲ 🛏
Ⅲ *safe (in some rooms)* 🍴 *Doc Dammers Bar & Grill* 🔊 🎵 ▣ 🎭 ♿ 🔋 ✕ ➕
🈲 ✕ ⊞ 🌙 📺 *1-800-THE-OMNI* @ www.omnihotels.com

A successful blend of new and old, with an emphasis on modern
conveniences, this historic hotel is popular with business travelers and
with wedding parties, too. Though it stands 13 elegant stories high, guest
rooms occupy only the top four floors. The oversized rooms feature
sitting areas, historic photographs, marble counters, gold-finished faucets,
and solid wood furnishings.

Hotel Place St Michel (43)
162 Alcazar Ave, Coral Gables, FL 33134
☎ **(305) 444-1666** ➡ **(305) 529-0074**

🚌 Bus 24, 37 *24 rooms* (and 3 suites) ●●● 📺 ▢ ⏲ *7am–10.30pm* ▣ 🖥
Ⅲ 🍴 *Restaurant Place St Michel* 🔊 🎵 ▣ 🎭 ♿ *banqueting room* 🈲
📺 *1-800-848-HOTEL* @ www.hotelplacestmichel.com

Built in 1926, this ivy-covered hotel in the heart of Coral Gables is one
of the city's most romantic options. With decor and hospitality straight
out of old-world Europe, it offers a quiet elegance that seems
welcomingly out of place in trendy Miami. Everything here is charming –
from the parquet floors to the paddle fans. No two rooms are alike, but
all have an eclectic mix of English or French furnishings, a small study
with a desk and some good books.

Not forgetting

■ **Hyatt Regency Coral Gables (44)** 50, Alhambra Plaza, Coral
Gables, FL 33134 ☎ (305) 441-1234 ➡ (305) 441-0520 ●●● *Opened in 1987
and inspired by the Alhambra in Granada, it has a Mediterranean feel.*

41

42

43

Coral Gables was created by George Merrick, the son of a Protestant pastor who came from New England at the beginning of the 20th century. Many of its buildings, such as the prestigious Biltmore Hotel, inspired by the Giralda Tower in Seville, are in the Mediterranean style.

44

Where to stay

Wyndham Grand Bay Hotel (45)

2669 S Bayshore Dr, Coconut Grove, FL 33133
☎ (305) 858-9600 ➡ (305) 858-4293

🚌 Bus 42 🅿 📶 *130 rooms (and 47 suites)* ●●●●● 🕭 extra ⬜ 🕐 ⬛ 🖥 ⅠⅡ⊧ 👥 Ⅲ safe 🍴 Bice 🎵 🔌 📺 💻 ✂ ♿ ➕ 📠 ≋ 🎾 🏛 📺 *1-800-327-2788* @ www.wyndham.com

With a silhouette like a Mayan temple and terraces covered in flowers, this hotel is easy to recognize. The lobby is decorated with Persian rugs, tropical plants and Chinese vases. Natural materials have been chosen for the naturally light bedrooms. A final touch of refinement is added by fine oil paintings and antique prints.

Grove Isle Club and Resort (46)

4 Grove Isle Dr, Coconut Grove, FL 33133
☎ (305) 858-8300 ➡ (305) 858-5908

🚌 Bus 12 *45 rooms (and 4 suites)* ●●●● 🕭 extra ⬜ 🕐 *7am–11pm* 🖥 📺 ⅠⅡ⊧ 👥 Ⅲ safe 🍴 Baleen 🔌 📺 💻 ✂ ♿ ➕ *banqueting room* ≋ 🎾 🏛 ★ 📺 *1-800-88GROVE* @ www.noblehousehotels.com

An island paradise. This sprawling complex with all the amenities of a country club is decorated with exotic frescos, mahogany furniture and pictures of monkeys, the hotel's emblem. The spacious, blonde-tone rooms each has a sitting area accented with kilims and its own terrace overlooking the sea.

Mayfair House Hotel (47)

3000 Florida Ave, Coconut Grove, FL 33133
☎ (305) 441-0000 ➡ (305) 441-1647

🚌 Bus 6, 27, 42, 48 🅿 📶 *179 rooms* ●●● 🕭 extra ⬜ 🕐 *6.30am–1am* ⬛ 🖥 👥 Ⅲ 🍴 *Mayfair Grill Restaurant* 🎵 🔌 🎭 📺 ✂ ♿ ✗ ➕ *banqueting room* ≋ 🏛 ★ 📺 *1-800-433-4555* @ www.mayfairhousehotel.com

A mixture of Spain and the Far East is enlivened by a touch of Art Nouveau in the heart of downtown Coconut Grove. All rooms are suites and include antique furnishings, marble bathrooms and hydro-massage tubs; some even include pianos and private Jacuzzis on their terraces.

Coconut Grove Bed & Breakfast (48)

P.O. Box 331891, Miami, FL 33233 ☎ (305) 665-2274 ➡ (305) 666-1186

🚌 Bus 37 🅿 *3 rooms* ●●● 🕭 ⬜ ⬛ 🖥 Ⅲ 💻 🏛 ★ 📺 *1-800-339-9430* @ www.kwflorida.com/coconut.html

An artist's house hidden in a secret location – the address is only divulged once you have a reservation; it is best to do this well in advance as there are only three rooms! The home, one of the earliest in Miami (1913), has an old-fashioned charm, with its period furniture, wood flooring, china, paintings by the owner and large bay windows which allow light to flood in...

Not forgetting

■ **The Mutiny Hotel (49)** 2951 S Bayshore Dr, Coconut Grove, FL 33133 ☎ (305) 441-2100 ➡ (305) 441-2822 ●●●● *Colonial-style entrance hall enhanced by warm-colored tiles and rooms with views over the bay and the park.*

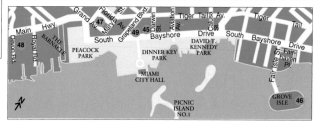

Coconut Grove was a fashionable bohemian area in the 1960s – Tennessee Williams and Robert Frost lived there. It is still considered a somewhat artsy area of Miami with sidewalk cafés, theaters and art galleries dotting its tree-lined streets.

Double tip

Some restaurants automatically add 15% service charge to the bill. The waiter does not always make this clear, so it is up to you to take care when you get the bill and, if necessary, add 15–20%, depending on the quality of the service.

Where to eat

Lexicon

Blackened: well cooked then flavored with a cajun sauce
Ceviche: fish marinated in lime and chilli
Chimichurri: hot Argentinian herb sauce
Gyoza: gnocchi stuffed with seafood and vegetables in stock
Jerk: Jamaican ground meat
Marlin: a small swordfish
Mojo: sauce with garlic and olives
Nori: marinated dried seaweed
Poblano: very hot Mexican chilli
Soba: Japanese black buckwheat noodles
Tempura: batter made from eggs, flour and water, for frying
Teriyaki: marinated in soy sauce, saké and ginger, before cooking
Tonno tetaki: cooked tuna chopped with onion
Vindaloo: Indian hot, spicy sauce
Wasabi: a condiment tasting rather like horseradish

The ever-changing gastronomic scene

In order to keep happy their fickle customers, who drift from one food fad to another, restaurants try to change constantly, by getting a new chef and a new name, redecorating, moving or re-thinking the menu.

Restaurants

THE INSIDER'S FAVORITES

INDEX BY TYPE

FIVE PRICE RANGES
- ● up to $ 15
- ●● $ 16-30
- ●●● $ 31-45
- ●●●● $ 46-60
- ●●●●● over $ 60

With 20 miles of coastline and dozens of islands, Miami has splendid panoramas wherever you happen to be: the sea and sky are the same clear blue, and the ubiquitous palm trees dot all the beaches. Strangely, few restaurants appreciate how to use this tropical beauty to their advantage. They do, however, understand that it should cost a little more

Where to eat

Red Fish Grill (1)
9610 Old Cutler Rd, Coral Gables, FL 33156
☎ **(305) 668-9975 ➡ (305) 668-8788**

🚌 *Bus 65* 🅿 *Fish and Caribbean* ●●● 🔲 🕐 *Tue.–Thu. 6pm–10pm; Fri.–Sun. 5pm–10pm* 🎦 🔰 ♿ ★ ☃ @ *redfishgrill@earthlink.net*

The Red Fish Grill, one of the most romantic spots in Miami, nestles inside the tropical greenery of Matheson Hammock Park, on the bay. As the name suggests, freshly caught fish, preferably grilled, is the main attraction in this establishment. Meat lovers needn't worry, however – they can get by quite happily with the Caribbean specialties such as the excellent spicy chicken.

Rusty Pelican (2)
3201 Rickenbacker Cswy, Key Biscayne, FL 33149
☎ **(305) 361-3818 ➡ (305) 361-7437**

🚌 *Bus B* 🅿 🍴 *Traditional and fish* ●●●● 🔲 🕐 *Mon.–Thu. 11.30am–4pm, 5pm–11pm; Fr.–Sat. 11.30am–4pm, 5pm–midnight; Sun. 10.30am–3pm, 5pm–11pm* 🎦 🔰 ▾ ♿ ★ ☃ @ *www.therustypelican.com*

An institution in Miami; the Rusty Pelican is famed as much for the quality of its food as for its rustic charm and breathtaking view of the sea. It caters for all tastes, from traditional fillets of beef, roast chicken or grilled fish to the more original fried whelks or alligator tail. You can drop in for a drink during the day to enjoy the comfort and the relaxing atmosphere overlooking the sea. A special children's menu for less than $10 is available: they can choose from spaghetti, pizza, meatballs, steak, grouper and grilled chicken.

Baleen (3)
4 Grove Isle Dr, Coconut Grove, FL 33133
☎ **(305) 860-4376 ➡ (305) 858-5908**

🚌 *Bus 12* 🍴 *Traditional and fish* ●●●●● 🔲 🍴 🕐 *Sun.–Thu. 7am–10pm; Fri., Sat. 7am–11pm* 🎦 🔰 ▾ 🌐 ♿ ★ ☃

You can expect a sophisticated meal, scandalously sensual ambience, high prices and slow service in this new restaurant belonging to chef Robin Haas, who already owns Grove Isle Club and Resort. The décor is country-style and there is a wonderful view over Biscayne Bay and Downtown from behind the white curtains draped between Moorish pillars. The carefully selected menu contains fish, oysters and crab (which have not always been caught in Florida waters). The fries deserve a special mention – long, crisp and served with salad or sandwiches at lunch time.

Not forgetting
■ **Tony Chan's Water Club (4)** Double Tree Grand Hotel, 1717 N Bayshore Dr, Miami, FL 33132 ☎ (305) 374-8888 Chinese ●●●● *Much appreciated for its fine cuisine and sea view.*
■ **Monty's Stone Crab/Seafood House (5)** 300 Alton Rd, Miami Beach, FL 33133 ☎ (305) 673-3444 Seafood ●●● *Magnificent vista over the harbor. Tasty crab in season (Oct.–May).*

to dine with a view at the water's edge!

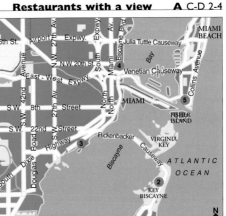

➡ Where to eat

Nemo (6)
100 Collins Ave, Miami Beach, FL 33139
☎ (305) 532-4550 ➡ (305) 532-4187

🚌 *Bus H, M; Electrowave* 🅿 *parking meters* 🔆 *evening* **Eclectic** ●●●● ▣ 🕐
*Mon.–Fri. noon–3pm, 7pm–midnight; Sat. 5pm–midnight; Sun. 11am–3pm,
6pm–11pm* ▥ ⬆ 🍸 ✳

An elegant spot – an Art-Deco palace restored with originality – in which
to savor eclectic cooking with oriental influences. Memorable dishes
include curried pork chops with onion *confit*, tuna with *nori*, Wasabi gelatine
and soy sauce.

China Grill (7)
404 Washington Ave, Miami Beach, FL 33139
☎ (305) 534-2211 ➡ (305) 534-2565

🚌 *Bus H; Electrowave* 🅿 *parking meters* 🔆 **World cuisine and oriental**
●●●●● ▣ 🕐 *Sun.–Thu. 11.45am–midnight; Fri., Sat. 11.45am–1am* ▥ ⬆ 🍸

Restaurant and disco. Always packed despite the high prices and rather
loud music. But the generous sized portions of fried spinach, lobster
fritters and mushroom pasta are worth a visit. A place to see and be seen
under the bright lights of South Beach.

Penrod's (8)
1 Ocean Dr, Miami Beach, FL 33139
☎ (305) 538-1111 ➡ (305) 534-8937

🚌 *Bus H; Electrowave* 🔆 **World cuisine and fish** ●●●● *Nikki Beach Club* ●●●
Penrod's Seafood ● *Deli Pizzeria* ▣ 🕐 *11am–11pm; Deli: winter and spring,
Mon.–Sun.; summer and autumn, weekends only* ▥ 🍸 ✳ 🔽

One bar, two elegant restaurants and a pizza stall all facing the ocean. The
Nikki Beach Club, the more fashionable restaurant, has very trendy staff
wearing short tops and sarongs to show off their tattoos! The second is
younger and more relaxed, offering a rather short but carefully prepared
'world' menu (chicken olives, *sushis*, crab and exotic salads).

Tap Tap (9)
819 5th St, Miami Beach, FL 33139 ☎ 305/672-2898 ➡ 305/672-0550

🚌 *Bus H; Electrowave* 🅿 *parking meters* **Haitian** ●● ▣ 🕐 *Mon.–Sat.
5pm–11pm, Sun. 5pm–10pm, (bar open until midnight)* ▥ ⬆ 🎵 *Thu., Sat.* 🍸

The murals, brightly colored paintings, live music and cheerful staff all help
create the happy atmosphere of this establishment, decorated in Haitian
colors. Rum punch and traditional dishes (squash soup, steamed
vegetables, fish with lime and lobster grilled with coconut).

Not forgetting

■ **Café Tabac (10)** 136 Collins Ave, Miami Beach, FL 33139
☎ (305) 695-8411 *Mediterranean* ●● *Simple Mediterranean dishes and
American-style lunch at reasonable prices. Terrace.*
■ **Tuscan Steak (11)** 433 Washington Ave, Miami Beach, FL 33139
☎ (305) 534-2233 *Italian* ●●●● *Family atmosphere.*

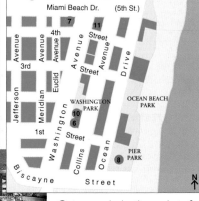

Gastronomy is also the product of the Miami melting pot: cooking takes on a little from each community... You are certain to be surprised by the subtle combinations.

Where to eat

Astor Place in the Astor Hotel (12)
956 Washington Ave, Miami Beach, FL 33139
☎ (305) 672-7217 ➥ (305) 672-7607

🚌 Bus C, H, K, W; Electrowave 🅿 parking meters 🍴 **New world cuisine, Mediterranean and oriental ●●●●●** ▢ ⊙ Mon.–Sat. 7.30am–11am; lunch: Mon.–Sat. 11.30am–2.30pm; dinner: Mon.–Thu. 7pm–11pm; Fri.–Sat. 7pm–midnight; Sun. 7am–11pm ⦚⦚⦚ 🍸 🛇 ⟊ @ www.astorhotel.com.

The gastronomic guru of Miami, Norman Van Aiken, keeps a close eye on the food at the Astor Hotel. Although busy with more media-oriented projects, including a television program, he still finds time to concoct amazing specialties such as 'chimichurri' grilled tuna with minced yucca or Vietnamese spring rolls on a bed of papaya.

Maiko Japanese Restaurant and Sushi Bar (13)
1255 Washington Ave, Miami Beach, FL 33139
☎ (305) 531-6369 ➥ (305) 672-2773 BEST

🚌 Bus C, H, K, W; Electrowave **Japanese** 🍴 ●●● ▢ ⊙ lun.-jeu. 12h00-0h00 ; Fri. noon–2am; Sat. 1pm–2am; Sun 1pm–midnight ⦚⦚⦚ ⟊

There is no better sushi at the center of South Beach. The tuna tetaki, the Californian rolls, the teriyaki and the gyosa are constantly replenished by the creative team of chefs working behind the counter. The décor is, frankly, nothing out of the ordinary, but the service is impeccable and the products very fresh. A regular, young clientele.

1220 and The Terrace at The Tides Hotel (14)
1220 Ocean Dr, Miami Beach, FL 33139
☎ (305) 604-5070 ➥ (305) 604-5182

🚌 Bus C, H, K, W; Electrowave 🅿 parking meters 🍴 1220 **French ●●●●●** The Terrace **Traditional ●●●** ⊙ 1220 Mon.–Fri. 7pm–11pm; Sat., Sun. 7pm–11pm; The Terrace Mon.–Fri. 7am–11pm: Sat., Sun. 7am–midnight ▢ ⦚⦚⦚ 🍸 🛇 ⟊ ✶ 🌿 🔽 1-800-OUTPOST @ www.islandoutpost.com

Sit on the Terrace at the Tides Hotel, contemplating the spectacle of Ocean Drive, in a bikini or a suit and tie. Inside at 1220 enjoy Paul Wade's simple, elegant creations inspired by French cuisine – pan-fried fillet of beef in red wine, mushroom risotto and exceptional desserts.

Not forgetting

■ **Mark's South Beach in the Nash Hotel (15)**, 1120 Collins Ave, Miami Beach, FL 33139 ☎ (305) 604-9050 Contemporary American ●●●●● Mark Militello, one of the best-known chefs in south Florida, offers imaginative dishes in an elegant, newly refurbished Art-Deco hotel.
■ **News Café (16)** 800 Ocean Dr, Miami Beach, FL 33139 ☎ (305) 538-6397 American ●● Café where you can try American specialties; busy all day.
■ **Grillfish (17)** 1444 Collins Ave, Miami Beach, FL 33139 ☎ (305) 538-9908 Fish ●●● A restaurant popular with Florida residents for its reasonable prices and elegant but welcoming décor

Japanese food is currently the 'in thing' in Miami. Presentation is always important, but quality does not suffer and dishes are constantly being updated.

Where to eat

Van Dyke Café (18)
846 Lincoln Rd, Miami Beach, FL 33139
☎ (305) 534-3600 ➡ (305) 534-3736

Bus M, R, S; Electrowave **American** ●● ○ *daily 8am–2am* @ www.newscafe.com

Sister establishment to the News Café in Ocean Drive. Pavement café/restaurant with simple, but good food (hamburgers and salads) to the accompaniment of live jazz. A few more elaborate meat and fish dishes. Always packed.

Pacific Time (19)
915 Lincoln Rd, Miami Beach, FL 33139
☎ (305) 534-5979 ➡ (305) 534-1607

Bus M, R, S; Electrowave **Asian** ●●●●● ○ *Sun.–Thu. 6pm–11pm; Fri., Sat. 6pm–midnight*

Without doubt the best restaurant of Miami Beach, the Pacific Time is expertly run by Jonathan Eismann whose know-how and originality are evident in all his dishes. The menu changes constantly, revolving around fish specialties such as grouper on a bed of shallots and grated ginger, sprinkled with saké and accompanied by *tempura* sweet potato fritters. For gourmands, the chocolate bombe, with melted chocolate, whipped cream and coulis of forest fruits, is divine!

Balans (20)
1022 Lincoln Rd, Miami Beach, FL 33139
☎ (305) 534-9191 ➡ (305) 604-9419

Bus M, R, S; Electrowave **international** ●● ○ *Sun.–Thu. 8am–midnight; Fri., Sat. 8am–1am* @ www.balans.co.uk

A strange atmosphere, reasonable prices and imaginative dishes in this establishment, straight from London. Noodles, club sandwiches with crayfish, pasta and salads; the ideal spot for a quick lunch or Sunday brunch.

Yuca (21)
501 Lincoln Rd, Miami Beach, FL 33139
☎ (305) 532-9822 ➡ (305) 673-8276

Bus C, G, H, K, L, M, R, S, W; Electrowave **Cuban nouvelle cuisine** ●●●● ○ *Sun.–Thu. noon–3pm, 6pm–11pm; Fr., Sat. noon–3pm, 6pm–midnight (summer schedule may close for lunch. Call to check)* @ www.yuca.com

Savor the flavors of the Caribbean prepared with American ingredients. Don't miss the crayfish medallions with sautéed spinach and stuffed mushrooms, preferably eaten outside or by the huge windows ...There is an unbeatable view of the goings-on in Lincoln Road.

Not forgetting
■ **Rosinella (22)** 525 Lincoln Rd, Miami Beach, FL 33139 ☎ (305) 672-8777 Italian ●● *Delicious pasta dishes served on the terrace* ■ **Bambu (23)** 1661 Meridian Ave, Miami Beach, FL 33139 ☎ (305) 531-4800 Asian ●●●●● *Excellent food and a nightclub atmosphere in this establishment, which is owned by the actress Cameron Diaz.*

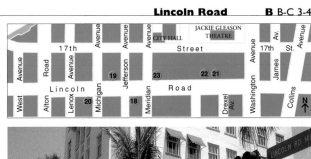

18

19

23

20

47

These restaurants have been chosen because they offer something different, be it strange décor, food with unusually subtle flavours, or a stream of colorful and eccentric characters; they may be sophisticated or decadent, but they all know how to combine the pleasures of the palate with entertainment and reveal the rather distinctive character of Miami.

▶ Where to eat

Blue Door (24)
1685 Collins Ave, Miami Beach, FL 33139
☎ (305) 674-6400 ➠ (305) 674-5649

🚌 Bus C, H, K; Electrowave 🍴 *French nouvelle cuisine* ●●●●● 🖥
🕐 7am–midnight ▥ 🔁 🍸 🚻 ♿ ✳

The Blue Door at the heart of the Hotel Delano gives its clientele of local celebrities a sophisticated but intimate location with first-class food. You must expect to pay extra for the stylishly elegant surroundings!

The Forge Restaurant (25)
432 Arthur Godfrey Rd, Miami Beach, FL 33140
☎ (305) 538-8533 ➠ (305) 538-7733

🚌 Bus C, J, K, M, T 🍴 *Traditional* ●●●●● 🖥 🍽 🕐 Fri.–Sat. 6pm–1am ▥
🔁 🍸 🎵 ♿ ✳

The Forge has been making a name for itself for thirty years with its welcoming décor, white-gloved waiters and faultless cuisine, beautifully complemented by the wine list with over 250,000 bottles from all over the world.

Joe's Stone Crab Restaurant (26)
11 Washington Ave, Miami Beach, FL 33139
☎ (305) 673-0365 ➠ (305) 673-0295

🚌 Bus H; Electrowave 🍴 *Traditional and fish* ●●●● 🖥 🕐 Tue.–Sat. 11.30am–2.30pm; Mon.–Thu. 5pm–10pm; Fri., Sat. 5pm–11pm; closed May 15–Oct. 15 ▥ 🔁 🍸 ♿ ✳ @ www.joesstonecrab.com

This has been setting the standard for seafood restaurants in Miami since 1913. Don't miss the rock crab in mustard sauce, hash browns, spinach with cream and garlic or onion *confit*. The only shadow on the horizon is that reservations are not taken, so you need to be patient to get a table.

Wolfie Cohen's Rascal House serves Jewish specialties at very reasonable prices day and night, in a typically American setting.

Chef Allen's (27)
19088 NE 29th Ave, Aventura, FL 33180
☎ (305) 935-2900 ➠ (305) 935-9062

🚌 Bus 3 🅿 🔲 New World ●●●●● ▭ 🍴 🕐 6pm–10pm Ⅲ 🔃 🍸 ♿ @
www.chefallen.com

Allen Susser has been amply rewarded for helping to invent Florida *nouvelle cuisine* and now offers a fantastic gastronomic experience. The elegant décor is very 70s, chrome and mirrors are everywhere and a large window enables customers to watch the chefs performing.

Not forgetting

■ **Tantra (28)** 1445 Pennsylvania Ave, Miami Beach, FL 33139 ☎ (305) 672-4765 Aphrodisiac cuisine ●●●●● *Real grass carpet and erotic sculptures. A place to meet up, or to finish off the evening. Good food, but service not always up to scratch.* ■ **Wolfie Cohen's Rascal House (29)** 17190 Collins Ave, Sunny Isles, FL 33139 ☎ (305) 947-4581 Jewish ● *The best Jewish specialties served at very reasonable prices day and night, in a typically American setting Sun.–Thu. 6.30am–2am; Fri.–Sat. 6.30am–3am.*

Where to eat

Hard Rock Café (30)
401 Biscayne Blvd, Miami, FL 33132
☎ (305) 377-3110 ➡ (305) 374-6058

Ⓜ Metrorail Ⓟ 🍴 American ●●● ▱ ◷ Sun.–Thu. 11.30am–11pm; Fri. 11am–midnight ▥ ▼ ♿ @ www.hardrock.com

The giant guitar above Bayside Marketplace is not an illusion; this is indeed the Miami branch of Hard Rock Café. Inside, as in all the others, are celebrity photographs and items which once belonged to rock 'n' roll stars ... Something exciting for the teenagers ... as long as they have not seen it all before in another branch. Slightly expensive for the type of food (mainly hamburgers); but you could find the ambience entertaining. Beware the decibels.

Big Fish (31)
**55 SW Miami Ave Rd. (5th St. 2 blocks west
of Brickell Ave.), FL 33130**
☎ (305) 373-1770 ➡ (305) 373-1770

Ⓜ Brickell Station Ⓟ Reserved Parking 🍴 Seafood/Italian ●●● ▱ ◷ Daily noon–3.30pm, 6.30pm–midnight; weekends noon–midnight ▥ ▨ ▼ ♿ ✶

Since a change in ownership in 2000, this waterfront hideaway serves surprisingly good Italian fare, including pastas, carpaccio, salads and, of course, fresh seafood. Even better though is the view along the gritty shores of the Miami River where Haitian tugboats and Coast Guard cutters cruise the inlet with the city's old buildings as the backdrop. It's popular with bankers and lawyers who come from nearby Bricknell Avenue at lunch and dinner. But is utterly casual. Most of the seating is outdoors, so check the weather before showing up. No reservations needed.

Fishbone Grille (32)
650 S Miami Ave, Miami, FL 33130
☎ (305) 530-1915 ➡ (305) 379-2545

Ⓜ Metrorail Ⓟ Fish ●●● ▱ ◷ Mon.–Fri. 11.30am–4pm; Mon.–Thu. 5.30pm–10pm; Fri., Sat. 5.30pm–11pm; closed Sun ▥ ▨ ▼ ♿

Miami residents appreciate the Fishbone Grille for its proximity to Tabacco Road, a traditional Miami meeting place; its rather unusual but still welcoming atmosphere; its cooking, based on freshly caught fish served with corn pancakes or other tasty accompaniments; its wine list, where you can unearth bottles (especially local wines) at reasonable prices; and for the décor, enlivened by a huge salt-water aquarium...

Not forgetting

■ **Diego's Tapas (33)** 401 Biscayne Blvd, R-104 (Bayside Marketplace), Miami, FL 33132 ☎ (305) 372-0072 Spanish ●● *Little tasting plates of shrimp in garlic, tortillas, croquettes, olives, salads, ham and cheese, and paella go well with sangria.* ■ **Morton's (34)** 1200 Brickell Ave, Miami, FL 33131 ☎ (305) 400-9990 American, meat ●●●●● *One of the best restaurants in town, specializing in meat dishes. Enjoy steaks with traditional American accompaniments. Subdued lighting and Chicago-style furniture give a warm, friendly atmosphere*

It is possible to find good little restaurants tucked in between discount computer stores and travel agencies or banks, beneath the imposing Downtown skyscrapers.

30

Where to eat

Stefano's (35)
24 Crandon Blvd, Key Biscayne, FL 33149
☎ (305) 361-7007 ➡ (305) 361-1681

▨ Bus B 🄳 week-ends **Northern Italian** ●●●● ▦ 🕐 5pm–11pm Ⅲ ♫ ♬ ☗ ৬ ☺ ✪ ★ @ www.stefanos.net

If there is a place to eat, drink and dance in Biscayne, this is it. You can even do a bit of shopping in the charming delicatessen and wine shop adjoining the restaurant... It is also your chance to dress up – most other restaurants on the island are more relaxed. The regulars take the opportunity of getting out their suits and ties. The cooking pays tribute to Italian traditions; service is a way of life in this establishment. Let yourself be tempted by the freshly caught fish, or the excellent risotto. There is a good wine list.

Sundays on the Bay (36)
5420 Crandon Blvd, Key Biscayne, FL 33149
☎ (305) 361-6777 ➡ (305) 361-8974

▨ Bus B **American** ●●● ▦ 🕐 11.30am–midnight Ⅲ ♫ ♬ ☗ ৬ ☺ ★ ✄

No one ever has second thoughts about coming down to Miami for a meal here on the water's edge, with a view over Downtown and Coconut Grove. On fine days it is especially pleasant to watch dolphins and walruses playing in the transparent water while you eat (particularly in the afternoons). The décor is tropical – wooden terrace, cane chairs and fans; the atmosphere becomes even more jolly with the arrival of reggae bands to warm up the proceedings.

Bayside Seafood Restaurant and Hidden Cove Bar (37)
3501 Rickenbacker Cswy, Key Biscayne, FL 33149
☎ (305) 361-0808 ➡ (305) 361-8884

▨ Bus B **Fish** ●● ▦ 🕐 Sun.–Thu. 11.30am–10pm; Fri., Sat. 11.30am–10.30pm (depending on weather) ♫ ♬ ☗ ☺ ★ ✄

An evening off the beaten track? Look no further than this Polynesian-style straw hut, renowned for its fish dishes. Freshly caught fish is indeed king here: grilled, fried, blackened, with smoked fish sauce, in fish cakes, sandwiches or soups... the choice is staggering! Do not expect too much in the way of service: the plates are plastic, and the serving staff not particularly attentive – they are more interested in current sporting events than earning tips. But the atmosphere at Bayside Seafood is very pleasant, especially at weekends when reggae or jazz groups add a sparkle to the evenings. The bar is open till 5am on Fridays and Saturdays.

Not forgetting
■ **Linda B. Steakhouse (38)** 320 Crandon Blvd, Key Biscayne, FL 33149 ☎ (305) 361-1111 American, meat ●●● *Intimate atmosphere enhanced by the pianist. A good spot if you want to eat meat in Key Biscayne.*

37

38

38

35

36

More than half Miami's inhabitants are Spanish speaking, coming originally from Cuba, South and Central America or other Caribbean countries. This has resulted in a wide variety of colors, customs and culinary traditions. Cuban *cafecitos*, Argentinian grills, Brazilian *rodizios* and Spanish *tapas* make Miami a city of intense *sabor*.

Where to eat

Larios on the Beach (39)
820 Ocean Dr, Miami Beach, FL 33139
☎ **(305) 532-9577** ➡ **(305) 531-5725**

🚌 Bus C, H, K, M, W; Electrowave 🍴 *Cuban* ●● ☐ 🕐 *Sun.–Thu. 11.30am–midnight; Fri., Sat. 11.30am–2am* 🎵 📋 🎶 🍷 👤 🔧

Pop star Gloria Estefan, a second generation Cuban-American, knows how to attract the crowds, as is shown by her concerts... and by her restaurant in Ocean Drive. A lively place to meet for lunch or dinner, Larios on the Beach offers Cuban specialties, such as *ceviche* (marinated fish) or roast pork with rice and red beans, at very reasonable prices.

Macarena (40)
1334 Washington Ave, Miami Beach, FL 33139
☎ **(305) 531-3440** ➡ **(305) 531-5925**

🚌 Bus C, H, K, M, W; Electrowave 🍴 *Spanish* ●●● ☐ 🕐 *Mon.–Fri. 12.30pm–3.30pm; Sun.–Tue. 7pm–midnight; Wed.–Sat. 7pm–1.30am (club open until 5am)* 🎵 📋 🎶 🍷

A must for the flamenco and classical guitar concerts. But the food is delicious too: *tapas*, pan-fried asparagus, stuffed mushrooms and paella delight the taste buds. Watch the sangria: it's deceptive!

Porcao (41)
801 Brickell Bay Dr, Miami, FL 33131
☎ **(305) 373-2777** ➡ **(305) 373-1177**

Ⓜ Metrorail 🍴 *Brazilian, meat* ●●●● ☐ 🕐 *noon–midnight* 🎵 📋 🍷 🔧 🌿 @ www.porcaousa.com

Brazilians flock to this amazing place... The beef, chicken or pork specialties will be prepared at the table, or you can help yourself to salads. A magnificent view and superb dessert menu add to the charm. If you eat like a sparrow, forget it!

Versailles (42)
3555 SW 8th St, Miami, FL 33135
☎ **(305) 444-0240** ➡ **(305) 444-4576**

🚌 Bus 8, 37 🅿 *Cuban* ●● ☐ 🕐 *9am–1am* 🎵 📋 🐾 🔧

Rather tacky décor, trying to look like France in the heart of Little Havana... but the food is undeniably Cuban, and includes a good *ropa vieja* (finely chopped beef). Good value for money: service a bit hit and miss.

Not forgetting

Casa Juancho (43) 2436 SW 8th St, Miami, FL 33135 ☎ (305) 642-2452 Spanish ●●● *Very popular with the Spanish community.*
■ **Tango Beef Café Argentinian Steak House (44)** 946 Normandy Dr, Miami Beach, FL 33139 ☎ (305) 861-7797 Argentinian ●●● *As the name suggests, this establishment is dedicated to meat: black pudding with soft bread, 20-ounce cowboy steak...*

Miami, a refuge for Cubans opposed to Castro, has also adopted the colors and flavors of Latin America into its food.

Where to eat

Norman's (45)
21 Almeria Ave, Coral Gables, FL 33134
☎ **(305) 446-6767** ➡ **(305) 446-7909**

🔲 Bus 24, 37, 40, 72 🔳 *New world* ●●●●● ▢ 🍴 ⏲ *Mon.–Sat. 6pm–10.30pm; closed Sun* ⅲ 🔳 ⓨ ⚬ @ www.normans.com

Everyone agrees that Norman's is one of the best restaurants in Miami. Not only for the elaborate cuisine displayed in the creative specialties, such as grouper with mojo spices, but also for the unbelievable wine list. Service is professional and courteous; the décor is elegant, luxurious but not ostentatious. The prices are obviously high, as you would expect in this class of restaurant.

Ortanique on the Mile (46)
278 Miracle Mile, Coral Gables, FL 33134
☎ **(305) 446-7710** ➡ **(305) 446-9895**

Ⓜ Metrorail 🔲 Bus 24 or 37 🔳 *Caribbean* ●●● ▢ ⏲ *Mon.–Fri. 11.30am–2.30pm; Mon.–Wed. 6pm–10pm; Thu.–Sat. 6pm–11pm; Sun. Oct.–April 5.30pm–9.30pm* ⅲ 🔳 ⓨ ⚬ @ www.ortanique@att.net

The ortanique is a Jamaican citrus fruit that tastes somewhat like a mandarin: this elegant restaurant is as original as the fruit whose name it bears. Its clientele is a mixture of well-dressed young businessmen and older customers who come after a movie to try the 'fusion' dishes created by chef Cindy Hutson: smoked marlin with papaya sauce, *penne* with *jerk* chicken in a creamy sauce and pan-fried blackened grouper; these are just some of the house specialties. For an especially romantic evening, ask for a quiet table: you will be tucked away under a diaphanous, almost gauzy, mosquito net the color of lemons.

Brasserie Les Halles (47)
2415 Ponce de Leon Blvd, Coral Gables, FL 33134
☎ **(305) 461-1099** ➡ **(305) 461-9912**

🔲 Bus 24, 37 *French bistro* ●●● ▢ ⏲ *11.30am–midnight* ⅲ 🔳 ⓨ ⚬ @ www.leshalles.com

Like any self-respecting brasserie, Les Halles will serve you until late in the evening; food is bistro-style (steak, salad, conserves and soufflés), and the atmosphere is relaxed, despite the brusque service (apparently typically French!). A good choice of wines. The only problem is the smoke which fills the rather cramped room and hides the posters of French movies covering the paneled walls.

Not forgetting

■ **Gables Diner (48)** 2320 Galiano Dr, Coral Gables, FL 33134 ☎ (305) 567-0330 American ●● *One of the last vestiges of Americanism. This restaurant serves well-produced food quickly and courteously. Its fans appreciate the traditional American dishes, such as meatballs in sauce and 'malts' (milkshakes with malt) at reasonable prices.*

Coral Gables was created in 1921, and was one of the first 'New Towns' of the United States. In the 1920s and 30s many of the new buildings were inspired by Spanish and Italian architecture of the 16th century. Miracle Mile is the queen of shopping streets: as the name suggests there is a mile of chic boutiques and quaint restaurants.

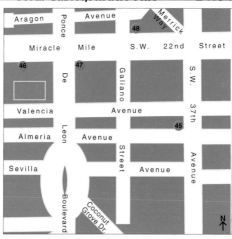

In the area

- ▸ **Where to stay:** ➡ 34
- ▸ **After dark:** ➡ 72
- ▸ **What to see:** ➡ 96
- ▸ **Where to shop:** ➡ 128

Where to eat

Caffè Abbracci (49)

318 Aragon Ave, Coral Gables, FL 33134
☎ (305) 441-0700 ➡ (305) 442-0061

🚌 Bus 24, 37 🅿 🔄 *Northern Italian* ●●● ▭ 🍴 🕐 *lunch: Mon.–Fri.
11.30am–3.30pm; dinner: Sun.–Thu. 6pm–11.30pm; Fri., Sat. 6pm–12.30am*
▥ 🔂 Ⓨ 🚻

This restaurant, tucked away in the heart of Coral Gables, pays tribute
to Italian traditions, particularly the specialties from the north. Always
packed and lively, it will continue serving until late into the evening. On
the menu are excellent pasta, risotto and fish dishes. Even on your first
visit, you will be welcomed like regulars by the proprietor Nino Pernetti,
who bends over backwards to satisfy his customers.

Miss Saigon Bistro (50)

146 Giralda Ave, Coral Gables, FL 33134
☎ 305/446-8006 ➡ 305/446-3085

🚌 Bus 24, 37, 40, 42 *Vietnamese* 🗂 ●● ▭ 🕐 *Mon.–Thu. 11.30am–10pm;
Fri., Sat. 4pm–11pm; Sun. 5pm–10pm* ▥ 🚻 @ www.misssaigonbistro.com

The room is small, but inviting, the waiters delightful, with a wonderful
sense of humor, and as for the food... without doubt the best Vietnamese
food in Miami. The keyword here is hospitality – you could be dining
with your best friends. This being the case, it is often full, so you may
well have to wait outside for a table. Your patience will be rewarded by
the oriental noodle soup, spring rolls or the spiced papaya salad –
definitely worth the wait.

Satchmo Blues Bar & Grill (51)

60 Merrick Way, Coral Gables, FL 33134
☎ (305) 774-1883 ➡ (305) 774-1528

🚌 Bus 24, 37 🕐 *American* ●●● ▭ 🕐 *Sun., Mon. 11am–1am; Tue–Sat
11am–2am* ▥ 🔂 Ⓨ 🚻 @ www.miamiblues.com

This is where to go in Coral Gables to recover after a day's work, have a
drink and a snack at the bar or listen to some music. The menu includes
calamari, chicken wings, hamburgers, fried fish served with potatoes, or
just soup and salad. The Satchmo is always busy (especially at weekends);
this is due more to the blues and jazz concerts (every evening) than to
the food or service, which can be slow.

The Globe (52)

377 Alhambra Circle, Coral Gables, FL 33134
☎ (305) 445-3555 ➡ (305) 445-6194

🚌 Bus 24, 37 🅿 *parcmètres* 🕐 *Eclectique* ●● ▭ 🕐 *Mon.–Thu.
11.30am–midnight; Fri. 11.30am–1am; Sat. 6.30pm–2am* ▥ 🔂 Ⓨ 🎵 🚻 ✴

This establishment doesn't serve great food, but pizzas, salads and
sandwiches in a pleasant relaxed atmosphere. Jazz concerts at weekends
in the evening are an attraction.

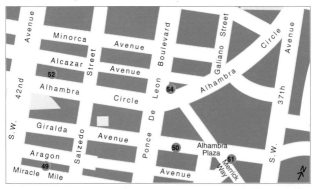

49

50

49

51

Alhambra Circle is to
business what Miracle
Mile is to shopping –
dozens of banks and
other multinationals have
opened branches here.
This explains why there
is such a large number
of restaurants.

In Miami it is impossible not to succumb to the tradition of Sunday brunch. Many hotels and restaurants offer great meals (scrambled eggs, *sushi* pasta, waffles etc.), washed down with champagne or cocktails, on their terraces. The best way to recover gently from the excesses of Saturday night...

Where to eat

The Courtyard Café at The Biltmore Hotel (53)
1200 Anastasia Ave, Coral Gables, FL 33134
☎ (305) 445-1926 ➡ (305) 913-3159

Ⓜ Metrorail 🚌 Bus 72 🅿 🍴 *Traditional and international* ●●●● ▣
🕐 *sittings Sun. 10.30am, 11.30am, 1pm, 2pm* 🎵 🎶 Ⓨ ⚫ ✴
@ www.biltmorehotel.com

Every Sunday the Mediterranean-style courtyard, surrounded by lush vegetation, swarms with crowds of hungry clients, proving that this is the best brunch in Miami. The tables groan with tasty food (omelettes – cooked to taste – pasta, waffles and tall glasses of colored ice-creams etc.), with as many cocktails as you want. Champagne flows... The price of $42 is the result, but this is the price of excellence. Reservations must be made well in advance.

Restaurant St. Michel (54)
162 Alcazar Ave, Coral Gables, FL 33134
☎ (305) 446-6572 ➡ (305) 529-0074

🚌 Bus 24, 37 *American nouvelle cuisine with French influences* ●●●
▣ 🕐 *Mon.–Fri. 7am–9.30am; Mon.–Sat. 11am–2.30pm: Sat.–Thu. 5.30pm–10.30pm; Fri. 5.30pm–11pm; brunch Sun. 11am–2.30pm* 🎵 🎶 🎶
Ⓨ ⚫ ♿ 📺 *1-800-848-HOTEL* @ *www.hotelplacestmichel.com*

In the lounge of a well-known hotel. Lace curtains and a romantic atmosphere add to the French charm of this rather quaint restaurant. Brunch costs $22.95 with champagne ad-lib and a selection of traditional dishes (eggs Benedict, omelette and waffles), as well as a buffet with meat, fish and tempting desserts. All to the strains of a talented pianist.

Island's Café (55)
9601 E Bay Harbor Dr, Bay Harbor Islands, FL 33154
☎ (305) 868-4141 ➡ (305) 867-9094

🚌 Bus G 🅿 🍴 *Traditional and international* ●● ▣ 🕐 *Tue.–Sun. 7.30am–9.30am, 11.30am–10pm, closed Mon.; brunch Sun. 11.30am–2.30pm* 🎵 🎶 🎶 Ⓨ ⚫ 🌿 @ *www.bayharborinn.com*

Used mostly by clients of the Bay Harbour Inn, who appreciate the café's location by the water's edge. As in the other meccas for brunch, you will be offered pasta, eggs, waffles, meat – and over twenty salads. The wonderful *ceviche* is recommended. Like the hotel, the restaurant is run by trainee hoteliers from Johnson and Wales University. A bargain at $19.95 per person.

Not forgetting

■ **Fontainebleu Hilton (56)** 4441 Collins Ave, Miami Beach, FL 33140 ☎ (305) 538-2000 Traditional and American ●●● *An unassuming steakhouse by night turns out a luxurious brunch every Sunday from 10am until 3pm for $32.*
■ **Bice Ristorante at the Wyndham Grand Bay (57)** 2669 S Bayshore Dr, Coconut Grove, FL 33133 ☎ (305) 860-0960 International ●●● *Quality brunch; as much ,sushi, crèpes and cocktails as you can manage, accompanied by a jazz trio, all for $38.*

In the area
- ▣ **Where to stay:** ➡ 36
- ▣ **After dark:** ➡ 72 ➡ 76
- ▣ **What to see:** ➡ 92
- ▣ **Where to shop:** ➡ 132

Where to eat

Anokha Fine Indian Cuisine (58)
3195 Commodore Plaza, Coconut Grove, FL 33133
☎ (786) 552-1030 ➡ (786) 552-0123

▣ Bus 27, 42, 48 **Indian** ▣ ●● ▣ ◯ *Tue.–Sun. 11.30am–2.30pm,
6pm–10.30pm* ▥ ▨ ▧ ★ @ *anokha.citysearch.com*

The tone is set by the ancient Sanskrit maxim on the menu '*Atitithi Devo
Bhava*': 'A guest is like God and should be treated accordingly'. The
proprietors Meena and Rohit Patel try to stick to this precept. The décor
is elegant, and the extraordinary traditional Indian dishes include lamb
samosas, mulligatawny soup (made from lentils, ginger and turmeric),
curried cauliflower and chicken *vindaloo*.

Monty's Restaurant and Rawbar (59)
2550 S Bayshore Dr, Coconut Grove, FL 33133
☎ (305) 858-1431 ➡ (305) 285-4273

▣ Bus 42 ▣ **Fish** ●●/●●●● ▣ ▮▮ *(restaurant)* ◯ *bar: Sun.–Thu.
11.30am–1am; Fri., Sat. 11.30am–2am; restaurant: Mon.–Fri. 11.30am–3.30pm
Sat., Sun. noon–3.30pm; Sun.–Thu. 5pm–11pm; Fri., Sat. 5pm–midnight* ▥ ▨ ♫
▨ ▧ ★ ❆ ▼ *1-800-817-3835 (to order crab by phone)* @
www.montysstonecrab.com

At the heart of Coconut Grove. A lovely view of the bay, an unbelievable
choice of food and cocktails at the ground floor bar, a popular meeting
place. The 'happy hour' in the evening is a must, and the concerts attract
crowds of people. The restaurant is famous for its Caesar salad, and its
crab (in season, Oct.–May). Courteous service.

Café tu tu tango (60)
CocoWalk, 3015 Grand Ave, Coconut Grove, FL 33133
☎ (305) 529-2222 ➡ (305) 461-5326

▣ Metrorail ▣ Bus 27 ▣ **Spanish and international** ▣ ●●● ▣ ◯
Sun.–Wed. 11.30am–midnight; Thu. 11.30am–1am; Fri., Sat. 11am–2.30am ▥
▨ ♫ ▨ ▧ ★ ❆ @ *www.cafetututango.com*

The paintings on the walls and resting on easels make you feel you are
in an artist's studio. You can eat mushroom soup with oriental *soba*
noodles, curried prawns with squash polenta, grilled chicken, pizza
poblano or cajun chicken olives in the strange *tapas* bar or in the second
floor restaurant. Customers of all ages meet here after work; cheap
drinks and concerts on Wednesdays.

Not forgetting
■ **Señor Frogs (61)** 3480 Main Hwy, Coconut Grove, FL 33133
☎ (305) 448-0999 ➡ (305) 529-9598 *Cuisine mexicaine* ●●● *Restaurant
and bar which holds riotous 'happy hours' when you can try delicious Mexican
specialties, iced margaritas and other special drinks*
■ **Green Street Café (62)** 3110 Commodore Plaza, Coconut Grove,
FL 33133 ☎ (305) 567-0662 *Cuisine classique* ●● *Pleasant open-air café on a
busy crossroads. Vast selection of salads, sandwiches and pasta.*

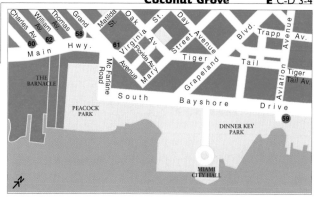

60

Coconut Grove still has a bohemian feel, its bars and restaurants retaining something of the hippie era.

60

62

61

59

Still open

Nightclubs come and go with disconcerting frequency... as if it were not enough that they close their doors for a 'private booking' without warning the public! Before setting out, call to check if the place you're heading to is still open.

After dark

Cafeterias

For a legal way to get a boost before heading out to a favorite club, try a shot of black gold. For about 50 cents, you can have a *cafecito*, a very strong coffee, very much like an Italian espresso. If you want enough to share with friends ask for a *colada*; for a coffee with steamed milk ask for a *cortadito*. You must also try straight sugar cane juice, *guarapa*, or the fresh coconut milk – the coconut is skillfully opened in front of you with a machete and you drink straight from it with a straw. Miami is packed with these little *cafeterias*, but the best ones are in little Havana, like **La Nara**, *1277 SW 8th St* ☎ *(305) 859-9909.*

Dance through the night – until tomorrow

Wanting to continue dancing longer than common sense dictates? Then you can find an 'after-after-hours' to carry on the wild dancing. The most famous after-hours in SoBe, a place that is usually full to the seams at nearly 7.30am, is **Mix**, *1417 Washington Ave, Miami Beach*
☎ *(305) 534-4717*
⏱ *Fri.–Sat. 4.30am–12.30pm*
● *$5/10.*

What to do in Miami?

To find out all about the restaurants, theaters, movie theaters, bars, clubs, auditoriums, festivals and other cultural events, it is vital to get hold of a copy of *The Miami Herald* Weekend section, which comes out on Fridays, *Street* or *New Times*.

35
Nights out
THE INSIDER'S FAVORITES

How To Get In

In SoBe (short for South Beach) the trendiest area of Miami, smart casual is the rule (neat but with a personal touch). Don't forget this when you are choosing your outfit. The best clubs have a rigorous selection process at the door. Baseball caps, shorts, T-shirts, jeans and sneakers are uniformly forbidden; make sure you impress the bouncer with trendy, elegant attire!

When visiting a hetero establishment it is best to come with a partner of the opposite sex, as they insist on the correct male/female ratio. For a better shot of getting into the A-list clubs, ask the hotel bellboy to put you on the guest list (expect to pay a tip of at least $20); it is the only way to get into the VIP lounge. Otherwise take your chances in the line up; however, if you are not in after half an hour, try elsewhere.

INDEX BY AREA AND TYPE

Dance clubs are open to everyone, but they do nevertheless tend to screen their clientele. It is vital to make a good impression on the doorman to get into the hotspots. It is worth the effort if you want to see American fashion icons and celebrities. Hence their luxury; some are more sophisticated and discreet than others... it all depends!

After dark

Lola Bar (1)
247 23rd St, Miami Beach, FL 33139
☎ (305) 695-8697 ➠ (305) 695-8699

🚌 Bus K; Electrowave 🕐 Nightly 9am–5am ● $20 ▣ Ⴤ @ www.lolabar.com

This sophisticated neighborhood club does no advertising; instead, it is a place for people in the know. With a steady and loyal following of locals and hip out-of-towners this off-the-beaten-path spot serves up a steady diet of great DJ mixes from ambient electronic to Eighties eclectic. White curtains separate the various different areas which contain pool tables, bedsize stools and long lounge chairs in an ultra cozy atmosphere.

Bash (2)
655 Washington Ave, Miami Beach, FL 33139
☎ (305) 538-2274 ➠ (305) 538-8858

🚌 Bus C, H, K, W; Electrowave 🅿 charge 🕐 Thu.–Sun. 10pm–5am ● $10/20 ▣ Ⴤ @ www.bashbarclub.com

An old-timer on South Beach, this intimate club has been hosting celebs and others for nearly a decade. The owners (celebrities themselves), Mick Hucknall of Simply Red and Sean Penn, might have glitzed it up but opted for elegance instead. The warmth of the wood and copper bar sets the tone as soon as you walk in. You can relax in the comfortable sofas in the VIP lounge on the mezzanine, peacefully watching people gyrating to the varied music (reggae, dance) on the main dance floor. Some will prefer the tranquillity of the Enchanted Garden; in the subdued atmosphere here it is easier to hold a conversation amid the gentle sound of world beat music and among the lush plants.

The Living Room (3)
671 Washington Ave, Miami Beach, FL 33139
☎ (305) 532-2340 ➠ (305) 532-1342

🚌 Bus C, H, K, W; Electrowave 🅿 charge 🕐 Tue.– Sun. 11pm–5am ● Tue.–Thu. $15; Fri., Sat. $20; Sun. $10 ▣ Ⴤ @ www.livingroom2000.com

For those who like the outrageous there is The Living Room, a very flashy club: you need only dance furiously to the dance rhythms, then go and finish your drink on a velvet sofa. For those who want to seduce and be seen, who are not put off by the extravagant luxury of the décor, which is over the top!

Not forgetting

■ **320 (4)** 320 Lincoln Road, Miami Beach, FL 33139 ☎ (305) 672-2882 🕐 Wed.–Sun. 10pm–5am ● $5/10 *Owned by local impresario Michael Capponi, this Lincoln Road hangout is the hotspot of the moment.* ■ **Bed (5)** 929 Washington Ave, Miami Beach, FL 33139 ☎ (305) 532-9070 🕐 Wed.–Sun. 8pm–1am ● entry free by invitation *Don't all good evenings end in bed? Reality is stranger than fiction... As the name suggests, at Bed you drink, eat and chat between dances stretched out on beds just like in Ancient Rome. Sofas, ottomans and elegant mattresses invite you to lie down in comfort, once you have removed your shoes and lined them up neatly.*

If you are looking for an intimate atmosphere, dance clubs are not for you! These huge establishments can hold more than 2,000 people: you are guaranteed a crowd. Huge clubs wage war with each other to attract night owls, as the running costs of these clubs are incredible. It is therefore vital to get a full house, by having the best DJs and artistic

After dark

Crobar (6)
1445 Washington Ave, Miami Beach, FL 33139
☎ (305) 531-8225 ➠ (305) 531-7066

🚌 Bus C, H, K, W; Electrowave ◷ Wed.–Sun. 11pm–5am ● $10/25 ▭ ⅄
@ www.crobarmiami.com

This fascinating place is tinged with genius; it conjures up the unlimited imagination of a Dali or Fellini. The Cameo movie theater – one of the cornerstones of Art Deco – has become, thanks to state-of-the-art technology brought straight from Chicago, a magical, dreamlike place. A DJ floating above the bar together with a heavenly host of angels, sculptures apparently hanging in mid-air, Harlequins on stilts; the strange world of Crobar is filled with so many people and objects. Giant fans on the walls create a kinetic sculpture of light and perpetual movement. Then, submerged in the dream world, you can lose your way in the maze of small lounges...

Level (7)
1235 Washington Ave, Miami Beach, FL 33139
☎ (305) 532-1525 ➠ (305) 695-9717

🚌 Bus C, H, K, W; Electrowave ◷ Mon., Thu.–Sun. 10pm–5am; Fri. gay ● $ 20
▭ ⅄ @ www.levelnightclub.com

This up-market newcomer to Miami nightlife was an immediate success. Its three luxuriously appointed stories are cleverly lit and teem with dance floors, bars and VIP lounges. Under the moving ceiling, which changes shape and breaks up the space, is the main stage. Whilst the regular nights at Level are obligatory for night owls and celebrities, it also stages huge special events and has become a national point of reference for fashion shows (Bulgari, Ralph Lauren) and other prestigious occasions.

Krave (8)
1203 Washington Ave, Miami Beach, FL 33139
☎ (305) 532-7279 ➠ (305) 532-5622

🚌 Bus C, H, K, W; Electrowave ◷ Mon., Tue., Fri., Sat. 11pm–5am ● $15

This relatively recent addition to SoBe's nightlife owes its popularity in large part to the entertainment put on in the VIP lounge; sometimes you could arrive to find yourself drowned in a downpour of soft white feathers...

Not forgetting

■ **Liquid (9)** 1439 Washington Ave, Miami Beach, FL 33139 ☎ (305) 532-9154 ◷ Thu.–Mon. 11pm–5am; Fri. gay ● variable *Elitism pushed to extremes always seems to pay. Huge lines at the entrance and selection, apparently based on Russian roulette, fail to deter the public. And to think they thought the 1980s were past!*

■ **Amnesia (10)** 136 Collins Ave, Miami Beach, FL 33139 ☎ (305) 531-5535 ◷ Thu.–Sun. 10pm–3am ● $5/20 *This open-air club attracts customers – particularly European tourists – and dazzles them with a multitude of laser or florescent light effects.*

directors to offer ever more spectacular programs and more audacious ideas than your competitors!

Generally, there is no skimping on all kinds of special effects in dance clubs. These huge palaces need to attract the crowds to cover the huge costs!

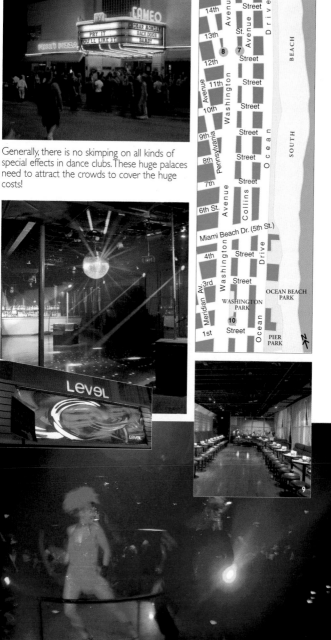

More intimate and relaxing than clubs, but just as popular, the lounge is an obligatory part of the long tropical night. There people meet friends, replay the last football game minute by minute, and discuss which club they will visit to round off the night. Usually there is no entry fee, and there are often free events. This phenomenon, which is currently very

After dark

Club Deuce (11)
222 14th St., Miami Beach, FL 33139
☎ (305) 673-9537 ➡ (305) 531-6200

🖼 *Bus C, H, K, W; Electrowave* 🅿 🕐 *8am–5am ● no credit cards*

For lovers of nostalgia, this is the place. Really nothing more than a seedy old bar, one of Miami's first, the Club Deuce is housed in a stunning single-story deco building designed by William Burbridge in 1926. These days it hosts bikers and billiard players, teachers and tattoo artists who come for cold beers or potent shots under the glow of crackling neon while Dean Martin and ol' Blue Eyes play on the juke box. With hours that begin at 8 in the morning, this is the ultimate after hours bar.

Blue (12)
222 Española Way, Miami Beach, FL 33139
☎ (305) 534-1009 ➡ (305) 672-1852

🖼 *Bus C, H, K, W; Electrowave* 🕐 *10pm–5am ● free* ▣ 🍸

A cocktail bar where everything from the décor to the lighting is monochromatic: here even life becomes 'blue'. On offer are fabulous parties, good-looking crowds and excellent DJs.

Twist (13)
1057 Washington Ave, Miami Beach, FL 33139
☎ (305) 538-9478 ➡ (305) 535-8317

🖼 *Bus C, H, K, W; Electrowave* 🕐 *1pm–5am ● free* ▣ 🍸

Twist, classified as wild entertainment, only gets going late in the evening. This two-story bar, with an outdoor patio, is a must-see for members of the gay community who want to know what Miami is really all about.

Score (14)
727 Lincoln Rd, Miami Beach, FL 33139
☎ (305) 535-1111 ➡ (305) 535-1164

🖼 *Bus G, L, M, S; Electrowave* 🅿 *nearby* 🕐 *3pm–5am ● free* ▣ 🍸
@ *www.scorebar.com*

Loud music in this strategically placed sidewalk bar on Lincoln Road with a perfect view over the happenings outside. It is also one of the best gay bars in Miami, open but elegant, attracting an upscale and youthful clientele. Its Sunday afternoon tea parties are particularly fashionable.

Not forgetting

■ **Penrod's South Beach (15)** | Ocean Dr, Miami Beach, FL 33139 ☎ (305) 538-1111 🕐 Daily: 11am–11pm except Fri. and Mon. until 5am. Variable ● *free. A ground-floor bar for those coming straight from the beach and another upstairs for customers with more in the way of clothing... Not typical of SoBe, this place attracts the crowds mainly with the 'Beehive', an evening which aims to encourage socializing.*

■ **Clevelander (16)** 1020 Ocean Dr, Miami Beach, FL 33139 ☎ (305) 531-3485 🕐 11am–5am ● *free. Very casual, ideal for those who do not want to dress up. On offer are music, live or with DJ, go-go girls and beauty contests.*

much in vogue, should become
more popular, considering the
prices and the benefits!

Lounge bars

13

16

Live music is one of the essential ingredients of Miami's nightlife. Bars where you can have a drink while listening to a set seem to be more common, reviving the best jazz and blues traditions of South Florida, which have been neglected recently. You might have to search but you can find world-class music around town.

After dark

Tobacco Road (17)
626 S Miami Ave, Miami, FL 33130
☎ (305) 374-1198 ➠ (305) 379-2545

Ⓜ *Metromover Brickell Outer Loop, 5th St.* 🔳 *Bus 8* 🅿 🕙 *noon–5pm* ● *$0/3* ⊟ 🍴 🍸 @ www.tobacco-road.com

A must. 100% made in America. Indifferent to any commercial logic or trends, Tobacco Road, the oldest bar in Miami, continues to promote blues, jazz and rock against all the odds. Relaxed and friendly, it is perfect for groups: an outstanding bar and a kitchen open until 2am offers good snacks at low prices. Two stories, a patio protected by a large oak tree and three stages.

Satchmo Blues Bar & Grill (18)
60 Merrick Way, Coral Gables, Miami FL 33134
☎ (305) 774-1883 ➠ (305) 774-1528

🔳 *Bus 24, 37* 🕙 *Tue.–Sat. 11am–2am; Sun., Mon. 11am–1am* ● *$0/10* ⊟ 🍸 @ www.miamiblues.com

The spirit of New Orleans comes to Miami's Coral Gables. Indoors or out, you can listen to live blues and jazz every evening (Monday Dixieland, Friday and Saturday blues) while sampling Cajun dishes. The establishment is quite large but still feels intimate.

Churchill's Hideaway (19)
5501 NE 2nd Ave, Miami, FL 33132
☎ (305) 757-1807 ➠ (305) 758-4481

🔳 *Bus 9, 10, 54* 🅿 🕙 *11am–3am* ● *$0/10* ⊟ 🍴 🍸 @ www.churchillspub.com

Very British! An authentic English pub transplanted into the heart of Little Haiti. It lacks nothing, not even the giant screen showing UK rugby and football matches. Hailed by the specialist press for over fifteen years as the best rock club in town, Churchill's has acted as a springboard for several artists (Mavericks, Marylin Manson...). Live bands from the local underground scene give spirited performances every evening. At mealtimes you can eat your fill of good food, washed down, of course, by draft beer.

Not forgetting

■ **Jazid (20)** 1342 Washington Ave, Miami Beach, FL 33139 ☎ (305) 673-9372 🕙 *9pm–5am* ● *$0/5 The intimate Jazid, where you could enjoy very good music (mainly jazz and blues) has been expanded. The program has improved as a result.*

■ **Power Studios & Poet Café (21)** 3701 NE 2nd Ave, Miami, FL 33137 ☎ (305) 576-1336 🕙 *Tue., Wed. 11.30am–2am, Thu.–Sun. 11.30am–3am* ● *variable At the heart of the Design District, a spacious up-and-coming club.*

■ **John Martin (22)** 253 Miracle Mile, Coral Gables, FL 33134 ☎ (305) 445-3777 🕙 *Sun.–Thu. 11.30am–midnight, Fri., Sat. 11.30am–1am* ● *free. Irish pub: friendly Irish folk. By the second beer, your feet are tapping, by the third you are dancing. Cabaret Saturdays.*

■ **Chili Pepper (23)** 2911 Grand Ave., Coconut Grove, FL 33133 ☎ (305) 442-2228 🕙 *Tue.–Sat. 9pm–5am* ● *$5/10 Garage bands, rock and alternative music at full volume.*

By day, the city sports a Latin attitude: from the cafés to the restaurants, from the radio to the shops, even the road layout. But by night, as if by some whim, it seems to forget this and relegates the Latin sound to the outskirts. You need to know where to look, but when you find it... an unforgettable night to the magical rhythms of the Caribbean and South America.

After dark

Starfish (24)
1427 West Ave, Miami Beach, FL 33139
☎ (305) 673-1717 ➡ (305) 534-8477

Bus M, S, W; Electrowave Fri., Sat. 9pm–4am ● $12
@ www.starfishsalsa.com

The house specialty is *salsa*. On Fridays there is a full house as live *salsa* takes over. Dancers of all ages, from novices to *salsa* veterans. You can come by yourself – there are plenty of willing *salsa* partners here. Starfish also organizes dance lessons.

Mango's Tropical Café (25)
900 Ocean Dr, Miami Beach, FL 33139
☎ (305) 673-4422 ➡ (305) 674-0311

Bus C, H, K, W, FLAGLER MAX; Electrowave charge charge 11am–5am (food 11am–4am) ● $5/10

The terrace opens on to Ocean Drive, but inside Latin-American music plays wildly every night. Full of life, very popular and always packed (could this be something to do with the waitresses' tiger-print lycra costumes?). People dance on the tables, in the street or on the dance floor. The frenzy is at its height on Tuesdays and Fridays on Brazilian nights.

Amnesia (26)
136 Collins Ave, Miami Beach, FL 33139
☎ (305) 531-7181 ➡ (305) 531-2345

Bus H, M, W; Electrowave Fri., Sat. 10pm–3am ● $10

Divided into several clubs including the Mojito Room, this is currently one of the most popular Latin-American haunts. This elegant establishment, where you dance under the stars, has earned its success by playing very good music.

Tropigala (27)
4441 Collins Ave, Miami Beach, FL 33139
☎ (305) 672-7469 ➡ (305) 672-0289

Bus G, H, J, L, S, T; Electrowave charge Wed., Thu., Sun. 7pm–midnight; Mon., Tue., Fri., Sat. 7pm–5am ● $15/20 @ www.clubtropigala.com

A reminder of a bygone age when Havana nights were animated by the casinos in the Cuban capital. On offer are dinner washed down with great wine, quality shows with dancers covered in sequins and feathers, and a band which is so lively you can't keep still.

Not forgetting

■ **La Covacha (28)** 10730 NW 25th St., Miami FL 33172 ☎ (305) 594-3717 Thu.–Sun. 5pm–4am ● $0/10 *Every Thursday (sushi happy hour), this night club fills up with a crowd of people who come straight from work to salsa. Friday and Saturday are Cuban nights; Sundays, rock – Latin American of course.*

■ **Illusiones (29)** 12540 SW 8th St, Miami, FL 33184 ☎ (305) 220-5705 9pm–5am ● $5/10 *Band or DJ, not just traditional salsa, but music from various trends in Latin-American music.*

25

27

24

27

Florida is the third largest cultural melting pot in the United States, after New York and Los Angeles, and is teeming with all kinds of artistic events from all backgrounds, some traditional, some avant-garde. But in Miami, music is the dominant force whether it be classical, orchestral, operatic, rock, Latin-American, jazz, blues or world.

After dark

Jackie Gleason Theater of the Performing Arts (30)
1700 Washington Ave, Miami Beach, FL 33139
☎ (305) 673-7300 ➠ (305) 538-6810

🚌 Bus C, G, H, K, L, M, R, S, W; Electrowave 🅿 charge 🕐 variable; box office: Mon.–Fri. 10am–5.30pm ● $17/150 ⊟ 🍸 @ www.gleasontheater.com

TOPA, an old television studio totally restored in the 1990s, is, with its huge seating capacity (2,700 seats), Miami Beach's main theater; it hosts classical ballets, Broadway shows and major productions. On the bill too are musical comedies such as *Footloose* and *Fame* and concerts by national and international pop stars. In addition, it regularly welcomes the Miami City Ballet and the Miami Grand Opera.

Colony Theater (31)
1040 Lincoln Rd, Miami Beach, FL 33139
☎ (305) 674-1026 ➠ (305) 534-5026

🚌 Bus A, M, R, S, W; Electrowave 🅿 charge 🕐 variable; box office: Tue.–Sat. noon–5pm and 1 hour before the show ● variable (approx. $20) ⊟ 🍸 🏨

This old Art-Deco movie theater (1934) has been carefully restored, and now successfully hosts smaller shows, ranging from theater to dance and classical music – the range of shows is vast. The Colony Theater is the base for the Rosa flamenco dance company.

Coconut Grove Playhouse (32)
3500 Main Hwy, Coconut Grove, Miami, FL 33133
☎ (305) 442-4000 ➠ (305) 444-6437

🚌 Bus 6, 22, 27, 42, 48 🅿 charge 🕐 variable; season: Oct.–May; box office: Tue.–Sat. 10am–8pm; Sun., Mon. 10am–5pm ● $ 35/40 ⊟ 🍸 @ www.cgplayhouse.com

This Rococo movie house was built in 1927 and converted into a theater. At the end of the 1950s, it hosted the American premiere of Samuel Beckett's *Waiting for Godot*. From that time, it has been famous nationally for its daring choice of productions. On the bill are original productions and classics, alternating with musicals.

Not forgetting

■ **Gusman Center for the Performing Arts (33)** 174 E Flagler St, Miami, FL 33131 ☎ (305) 374-2444 🕐 variable; season: Oct.–June; box office: Mon.–Fri. noon–2.30pm, 3pm–5.30pm and 2 hours before the show ● $18,50/75 *Dating from 1926, it plays host to the Miami Film Festival, concerts given by the Florida Philharmonic and other musical events.*
■ **Dade County Auditorium (34)** 2901 W Flagler St., Miami, FL 33135 ☎ (305) 547-5414 🕐 variable; box office: Mon.–Fri. 9am–4pm and 1 hour before the show ● $12/130 *It was built in 1951, and three years later welcomed a still unknown Luciano Pavarotti... Thanks to its excellent acoustics, multifunctional layout and 2,400 seats, international companies touring the United States often visit.*
■ **Lincoln Theater (35)** 541 Lincoln Rd, Miami Beach, FL 33139 ☎ (305) 673-3331 🕐 variable; season: Oct.–May; box office: Mon.–Fri. 10am–5pm and 1 hour before the show ● $10/60 *The New World Symphony Orchestra, a prestigious local group, opens its new season in this charming Art-Deco theater.*

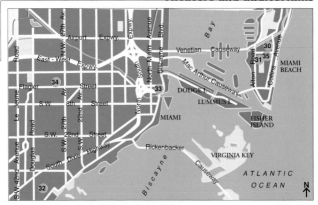

Art Deco Street Festival

In mid-January, Ocean Drive and the surrounding area pay tribute to the key architectural style of Miami Beach, Art Deco. Period cars and decorative objects, food kiosks and open-air concerts surround one of the nicest diversions in the city for three days. For information ☎ (305) 672-2014.

What to see

Design District

The Design District is located between Little Haiti and Downtown. This area has found a new lease of life thanks to the artists, designers, photographers, interior designers and architects who moved here from overpriced South Beach. They have renovated it and succeeded in making it into an artistic urban laboratory that is something out of the ordinary.

Discovering the Deco District

In the Art Deco Welcome Center you will find leaflets, gadgets, bikes to rent and suggestions for interesting guided tours of the Art-Deco area of South Beach. **Miami Design Preservation League**, *Ocean Front Auditorium, 1001 Ocean Dr, Miami Beach, FL 33139* ☎ *(305) 672-2014* ◙ *Mon.–Wed. 11am–6pm; Thu.–Sun. 11am–11pm.*

71
Sights
THE INSIDER'S FAVORITES

Festivals of every description

The different cultures that make Miami a multi-ethnic capital can be seen in arts, crafts and cuisine... They are also celebrated during the festivals which take place throughout the year: Latin-American in March, during the Carnival Miami Festival which culminates in an open-air festival attracting a million people to Calle Ocho; Caribbean in October with the Indian Carnival; African-American in November with the Sunstreet Carnival. There are also big sporting events: Mid-Winter Sailing Regatta, Miami Grand Prix (motor racing), Doral Ryder Open (golf), Royal Caribbean Open (golf). For more information see the *Miami Herald* or the *New Times*.

A megalopolis has taken over an area that not long ago was mosquito-infested mangrove swamps. What was once a fishing village is now a holiday destination valued by tourists from all over the world for its miles of white, sandy beaches, temperate climate and lively nightlife.

What to see

(2) ➡ 82

(15-27) ➡ 86

(32) ➡ 88

(34) ➡ 88

(38) ➡ 90

The Wolfsonian Foundation ➡ **82**
A fascinating museum of late 19th–mid 20th century art and artifacts, emphasizing propaganda arts.

Deco District ➡ **86**
The triumph of "Tropical" Art Deco. The largest protected architectural district in the United States.

NationsBank Building ➡ **88**
This skyscraper has become the symbol of Miami.

Atlantis ➡ **88**
An odd, cutout building that owes its fame to the TV series "Miami Vice". The rather outrageous architects at Arquitectonica designed it.

Ancient Spanish Monastery ➡ **90**
Authentic 12th-century monastery, bought in Spain, painstakingly dismantled, transported to America, and rebuilt piece by piece in 1952.

Vizcaya Museum and Gardens ➡ **92**
The industrialist James Deering, a great art-lover,

had this luxurious neo-Renaissance villa built between 1911 and 1916. It is now the property of the city of Miami.

Fairchild Tropical Garden ➡ **94**
The largest tropical botanical garden in the United States, with more than 83 acres of exotic plants.

Coral Castle ➡ **94**
The work of a Latvian refugee, who obsessively sculpted the coral in honor of the woman he loved.

The Biltmore Hotel ➡ **96**
The Biltmore is one of the most famous and luxurious hotels in Miami. Opened in 1926, its Spanish neo-Renaissance architecture has housed dozens of celebrities, ghosts, and an Al Capone's speakeasy.

The beaches of Miami Beach ➡ **98**
The beaches are part of the myth of Miami; they spread as far as the eye can see, and swarm with people all year round.

(42) ➡ 92

(46) ➡ 94

(48) ➡ 94

(53) ➡ 96

(63-66) ➡ 98

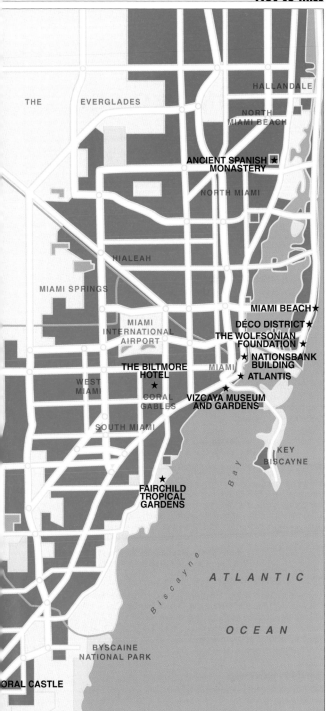

In the area
 Where to stay: ➡ 18 ➡ 20 ➡ 26
 Where to eat: ➡ 42 ➡ 44 ➡ 48 ➡ 54
 After dark: ➡ 66 ➡ 68 ➡ 70 ➡ 74
 Where to shop: ➡ 116

What to see

Sanford L Ziff Jewish Museum (1)
301 Washington Ave, Miami Beach, FL 33139
☎ (305) 672-5044 ➡ (305) 672-5933

Bus C, H, K, M, W; Electrowave Tue.–Sun. 10am–5pm; closed Jewish holidays ● $5 adults; $4 concessions; Sat. free
www.jewishmuseum.com

A 1936 deco-style building (formerly the city's first Orthodox synagogue) houses this tribute to 230-plus years of Jewish history in Florida. Dozens of stained glass windows, business cards from Jewish companies, a marble bimah (the podium for the Torah), photographs, and other icons of frequently persecuted lives are displayed.

The Wolfsonian Foundation (2)
1001 Washington Ave, Miami Beach, FL 33139
☎ (305) 531-1001 ➡ (305) 531-2133

Bus C, H, K, W Mon., Tue., Fri., Sat. 11am–6pm; Thu. 11am–9pm; Sun. noon–5pm; closed Christmas and New Year ● $5 adults; $3.50 concessions English, Spanish: times variable @ www.wolfsonian.org

When Mitchell Wolfson, Jnr's collection of late 19th–mid 20th Century artifacts grew too large (more than 70,000 pieces), he bought the Mediterranean-style building where they were stored, and converted it into this spectacular space. Exhibits of model trains, furniture, posters, and hundreds of everyday objects provoke thought and emotional responses, questioning the purposes of design and the media, their influence and power.

Amsterdam Palace (3)
1114 Ocean Drive, Miami Beach, FL 33139

Bus C, H, K, W; Electrowave not open to the public

It was on the steps of this magnificent mansion that Gianni Versace was murdered in 1997. Earlier in the decade, he bought and lovingly restored the architectural marvel – rumored to be an exact replica of Christopher Columbus's childhood home – adding his trademark ornate designs throughout. It remains primarily hidden behind immense gates and walls.

Estefan Enterprises (4)
420 Jefferson Ave, Miami Beach, FL 33139

Bus C, K, M Parking meters not open to the public

The whimsical building, designed by the world-famous Arquitectonica, houses the offices of Emilio and Gloria Estefan's entertainment empire. Its façade is carved with color-lined waves and fanciful shapes. Metal doors that evoke the tropics, an oasis shaped roof that has trees growing from it, and other whimsical touches make this building an appropriately modern addition to the deco district.

Not forgetting
■ **South Pointe Park (5)** from dawn to dusk. This charming little park on the southernmost tip of Miami Beach is the perfect place to sit and watch behemoth cruise ships enter and depart the port of Miami.

Before it was turned into a museum, rich Miami residents used the Wolfsonian Foundation building as a furniture storehouse.

83

What to see

Miami Beach Post Office (6)
1300 Washington Ave, Miami Beach, FL 33139

🚌 Bus C, H, K, W; Electrowave 🅿 🕐 Mon.–Fri. 8am–5pm; Sat. 8.30am–2pm; closed public holidays ♿ 📺 1-800-275-8777

Built in 1937, this landmark building catches the eye with its beautiful rotunda and coral stairs. An intricate sun motif surrounds the lantern on the ceiling, which illuminates the epic mural depicting the expeditions of Ponce de Leon in 1513 and his confrontations with Indians.

Bass Museum (7)
2121 Park Ave, Miami Beach, FL 33140 ☎ (305) 673-7530

🚌 Bus H ,K, C 🅿 parking meters 🕐 Tue.–Sat. 10am–5pm; Sun. 1pm–5pm; 2nd and 4th Wed. of the month 10am–9pm, closed Christmas ● $5 adults; $3 senior citizens and students 🍴 🎫 🏛 ♿

The Bass Museum reopened late in 2000, following renovations and physical expansion. The museum boasts one of the finest collections of tapestries in the U.S. Its permanent collection spans the millennium, with works from the Old Masters, Renaissance, and Modern artists.

Holocaust Memorial (8)
1933 Meridian Ave, Miami Beach, FL 33139 ☎ (305) 538-1663

🚌 Bus G, L, M, S; Electrowave 🅿 parking meters 🕐 9am–9pm ● free 🏛 ♿

One of the most powerful images anywhere, the centerpiece of the Holocaust Memorial is The Sculpture of Love & Anguish, a giant, yearning hand covered with victims of the concentration camps and an Auschwitz number tattoo. But don't stop there. Beneath it rests a solemn tableau of bronze victims lying strewn across the floor. Along the reflecting pool, the carved marble walls tell the story of the Holocaust.

The Mermaid Sculpture (9)
1700 Washington Ave, Miami Beach, FL 33139

🚌 Bus G, K, L, M, S, W; Electrowave

This pop art masterpiece from Roy Lichtenstein – best known for his comic strip-like paintings – sits before the Jackie Gleason Theater. Its playful, suggestive lines capture the ebullient spirit of Miami Beach

Not forgetting

■ **Española Way (10)** (between Washington and Drexel Aves) (10) Modeled after a small Spanish Village, this one block of Española Way was established as an artists' community. Today, its quaint charm houses a variety of shops, restaurants, residences, and studios. ■ **Lincoln Mall (11)** Take a walk along this pedestrian mall to admire Morris Lapidus's series of angular, whimsical, and puzzling sculptures (between Washington Ave and Linton Blvd) or the magnificent Art-Deco buildings such as the Colony Theater (no. 1040), the glass-block/blue neon faced Sterling Building (no. 927) or the Lincoln Theater (no. 555) and its tropical motifs. ■ **Miami Beach (12–14)** is home to some of the most beautiful pools in the country. (12–14) The Albion Hotel's (12), 1650 James Ave, pool has its viewing portholes; the Delano's (13), 1685 Collins Ave, tables and chairs seem to float in the water; and the Raleigh's (14), 1775 Collins Ave, draws the eye with exquisite lines and waterfalls.

Art Deco began in Paris in 1925, and took on a particular form in Florida, which became known as Tropical Deco: pastel colors, neon lights and original decorative motifs (flamingos, roses, egrets and pelicans) covered façades, as if to cock a snook at the great depression which had seized the country. The main buildings in Miami Beach were the works

What to see

Deco District (15-27)
**Information: Art Deco Welcome Center,
1001 Ocean Drive, Miami Beach,
FL 33139 ☎ (305) 531-3484**

C, H, K, W; Electrowave **Miami Design Preservation League**, *guided walking tours of the district* *Thu. 6.30pm, Sat. 10.30am* ● *$10 adults; $7 concessions*

The image of Miami Beach is inextricably linked to fashion, nightlife, sun and beaches... and Art-Deco architecture, known here as 'Tropical Deco'. This architectural style is characterized by pastel colors evocative of the mild climate, elegant lines enlivened by porthole windows, is enhanced by neon lighting and decorated by bas-reliefs with themes from mythology or the aquatic world. The almost 800 buildings in the Deco District recorded in the National Register of Historic Monuments make Miami Beach one of the largest architectural areas to be protected by the United Nations with the highest concentration of Art-Deco buildings in the world. Officially the district stretches between Dade Blvd to the north, 6th St. to the south, the Atlantic Ocean to the east and Lennox Ave to the west. The most interesting buildings, however, are to be found on Ocean Drive and Collins Ave, and you need to see them at different times of the day. Daylight gives life to the colors; at night the neon and other artificial lights suffuse the buildings with a ghostly halo. The Century Hotel **(15)**, the most Mediterranean of the architectural gems in the district (140 Ocean Drive), is distinguished by its aerodynamic lines and mint-green color. The historic façade of Gallery Hotel **(16)**, at no. 444, is decorated with bas-reliefs featuring tropical plants, sea birds and nudes, whereas the Park Central **(17)** at no. 640, by

of Hohauser, Anis Skislewicz or Murray Dixon, who left their mark on the Deco District between 1934 and 1941.

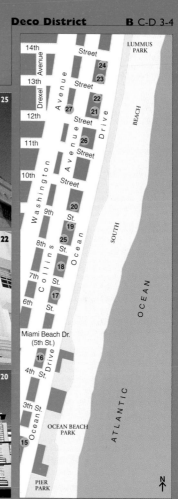

Hohauser, can be recognized by its octagonal portholes and angled windows. The famous neon signs of the Hotel Colony **(18)** at no. 736 have starred in dozens of movies and television series. The ornamental lighthouse on the roof of the Waldorf Towers, a little way along the road **(19)**, takes you by surprise. The central tower on the Breakwater Hotel **(20)**, the work of Anton Skislewicz (no.900), is reminiscent of a ship's funnel or a totem pole. No. 1220, The Tides **(21)**, is like an austere spaceship that has just landed... Next is the Hotel Leslie **(22)** at no. 1244, with the pilasters and bright yellow façade, followed by the more futuristic Cardozo **(23)**, no. 1300, recognizable by the veranda with the coral balustrade. A bit further along, at no. 1330, the huge Netherland **(24)** marries monumental architecture and a love of detail, from the staircase fountain to the grandiose terrace. At no. 801 Collins Ave can be seen the pinnacle of the Tiffany, alias The Hotel **(25)**, recently restored by designer Todd Oldham. The Hotel Kent **(26)**, at no. 1131 Collins Ave, also stands out because of its pinnacle. The Marlin**(27)**, 1200 Collins Ave, with its neon borders, is considered one of the best examples of Tropical Deco **(440)**.

What to see

Miami Art Museum (MAM) (28)
Metro-Dade Cultural Center, 101 West Flagler St., Miami, FL
33130
☎ **(305) 375-3000** ➠ **(305) 375-1725**

Ⓜ *Metrorail and Metromover, Government Center* 🚌 *Bus C, K, S, T, 2, 3, 9, 10, 16,
21* 🅿 *$2* 🕐 *Tue.–Fri. 10am–5pm; 3rd Thu. of the month 10am–9pm; Sat., Sun.
noon–5pm; closed Thanksgiving, Christmas and New Year* ● *$5 adults; $2.50 senior
citizens and students* ▭ 🈂 *Tue.–Fri. English and Spanish by appointment* 🈵 ♿
@ *www.miamiartmuseum.org*

The world's most important exhibitions travel to MAM, which only
recently acquired a permanent collection. Expertly curated and fascinatingly
notated, the exhibits tend to focus on subjects of local and regional
interest. Caribbean artists, both schooled and naïve, are often featured.

Historical Museum of Southern Florida (29)
Metro-Dade Cultural Center, 101 West Flagler St., Miami, FL
33130
☎ **(305) 375-1492** ➠ **(305) 375-1609**

Ⓜ *Metrorail and Metromover, Government Center* 🚌 *Bus C, K, S, T, 2, 3, 9, 10, 16,
21* 🅿 *$2* 🕐 *Mon., Wed., Fri., Sat. 10am–5pm; Tue. 10am–9pm; Sun. noon–5pm;
closed Thanksgiving, Christmas and New Year* ● *$5 adults; $4 concessions; $2 for 6–
12 years* ▭ 🈂 *museum and town: variable* 🈵 ♿ @ *www.historical-museum.org*

Permanent exhibitions trace the history of Miami from pre-historic
times, spotlighting its rich cultural heritage (e.g. Seminole culture, Spanish
colonization and the city's founding).

Bayfront Park (30)
301 N Biscayne Blvd, Miami, FL 33132

Ⓜ *Metromover, College/Bayside* 🚌 *Bus C, S, T, 3, 16* 🅿 🚼 🕐 *dawn to dusk*

An oasis of green in the middle of downtown, Bayfront Park was founded
in 1924 and redesigned in 1987 by Isamo Noguchi, creating a 'wedge of art
into the heart of the New World'.

Not forgetting

■ **Miami Public Library - Main Branch (31)** *Metro-Dade Cultural
Center, 101 W Flagler St., Miami, FL 33130* ☎ *(305) 375-2665* 🕐 *Mon.–Wed.,
Fri. 9am–5pm; Thu. 9am–9pm; Sat. 9am–6pm; Sun. 1pm–5pm; closed public
holidays and Sun. end May-Sep. Two dynamic art galleries with frequently changing
exhibitions.* ■ **NationsBank Building (32)** *100 SE 1st St., Miami, FL
33132 At night, horizontal bands of colored light run across the I.M. Pei designed
building from top to bottom* ■ **The Freedom Tower (33)** *600 Biscayne
Blvd, Miami, FL 33132 This tower was constructed in 1932, taking much inspiration
from La Giralda in Seville. The home of the Miami Daily News for 32 years, it
became the reception center for Cuban refugees in the 1960s.* ■ **Atlantis (34)**
*2025 Brickell Ave, Miami, FL 33132 This amazing building 'with a hole in the
middle' was designed by Arquitectonica and has become famous throughout the
world thanks to the TV series "Miami Vice".* ■ **US Federal Courthouse
(35)** *300 NE 1st Ave, Miami, FL 33132* ☎ *(305) 536-4548* 🕐 *Mon.–Fri.
9am–5pm In the main room on the second floor of this neoclassical edifice built in
1931 is a mural by Denman Fink depicting the history of Miami and Florida from
their origins to the present day.*

Since the boom of the 1980s, neoclassical (early 20th-century) and Art-Deco buildings have been standing side by side with the most audacious skyscrapers.

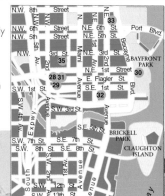

In the area
- **Where to stay:** ➡ 28 ➡ 32
- **Where to eat:** ➡ 48 ➡ 49 ➡ 54 ➡ 60
- **After dark:** ➡ 72
- **Where to shop:** ➡ 120 ➡ 124

What to see

Bacardi Import Headquarters (36)
2100 Biscayne Blvd, Miami, FL 33137 ☎ (305) 573-8511

🚌 Bus T, 3, 16, 36, 36 A, 62 🕐 *by appointment only, Mon.–Fri. 9am–5pm; closed public holidays* ● *free* ♿

This building's fantastic mosaic façade is a towering burst of art along an otherwise drab stretch of road. This headquarters of the famous rum-distiller contains a little museum retracing, by means of photos, paintings and sculptures by family members, the history of the family and the company from its founding in 1838.

American Police Hall of Fame and Police Museum (37)
3801 Biscayne Blvd, Miami, FL 33137
☎ (305) 573-0070 ➡ (305) 573-9819

🚌 Bus T, 3, 16, 36, 36 A, 62 🅿 🕐 *daily 10am–5.30pm; closed Thanksgiving, Christmas* ● *$6 adults; $4 over-65s; $3 for 0-12; $0.25 Miami police; $1 other police* ⬛ 🔲 *groups of over 20* ⊞ ♿ @ *www.aphf.org*

This odd museum boasts such exhibits as a rogue's gallery of criminals and an array of handcuffs, batons, and other police tools. A tribute to the many officers who have died on duty offers a solemn reminder of the museum's significance.

Ancient Spanish Monastery (38)
16711 W Dixie Hwy, North Miami Beach, FL 33160
☎ (305) 945-1461

🚌 Bus E, H, V, 3, 83 🅿 🕐 *Mon.–Sat. 10am–4pm; Sun. 1pm–5pm* ● *$4.50 adults; $2.50 over-55s and students; $1 for 3–12 years* ⬛ 🔲 *telephone for groups of over 12 persons* ⊞ ♿ @ *www.floridagoldcoast.com www.spanishmonastery.com*

The oldest building in the Western Hemisphere, this magnificent structure was built in 1141, in Segovia, Spain. Newspaper magnate, William Randolph Hearst purchased the building and had it disassembled, crated, and shipped block by block to New York en route to his California Estate. Unfortunately, Segovia was suffering an outbreak of cattle disease, and the entire 11,000 crates were quarantined in New York... for 26 years. In 1952 two entrepreneurs decided to purchase and assemble 'the biggest and most expensive puzzle in the world'. They managed it: gorgeous stained glass, statuary, carvings, and paintings all seem to have found their rightful places. A tranquility surrounds the locale which still holds Sunday mass at 8.00 and 10.30 am.

Not forgetting

■ **Museum of Contemporary Art (MoCA) (39)** 770 NE 125th St, North Miami, FL 33161 ☎ (305) 893-6211 🕐 Tue.–Sat. 11am–5pm; Sun. noon–5pm; closed Thanksgiving. Christmas and New Year ● $5; $3 concessions. *Dedicated to the work of 20th- (and 21st-) century artists, MoCA houses both permanent and traveling exhibits, both internationally recognized artists and regional visionaries, in its 23,000 square feet.* ■ **Greynolds Park (40)** 17530 W Dixie Hwy, North Miami Beach, FL 33160 ☎ (305) 945-3425 🕐 dawn to dusk. *This oasis combines mangroves with bike trails, picnic tables with grassy hills, hidden away behind the busy West Dixie Highway.*

36

38

39

39

What to see

Miami Seaquarium (41)
4400 Rickenbacker Cswy, Virginia Key, FL 33149
☎ **(305) 361-5705** ➔ **(305) 361-6077**

🔲 *Bus B* 🅿 🔲 $ 4 🕙 9.30am–6pm ● $21.95; $16.95 concessions; **Swim with the dolphins** $125 🔲 🔲 🔲 🔲 🔲 @ www.miamiseaquarium.com

Simultaneously cheesy and fascinating, the Miami Seaquarium remains a Miami institution, with thousands of fish of all sizes, shapes, and colors. The television show, Flipper was filmed here, and trained dolphins still swim in that cove. Dolphins, sea lions, and Lolita the killer whale perform fun shows throughout the day (be sure and sit at least 10 rows back if you want to stay dry).

Vizcaya Museum and Gardens (42)
3251 S Miami Ave, Miami, FL 33129 ☎ **(305) 250-9133**

🔲 *Bus 12, 48* 🅿 🕙 daily 9.30am–4.30pm ● $10; $5 for 6–12 years 🔲 🔲 🔲 🔲 🔲 🔲

It took 1,000 artisans five years to complete this magnificent mansion, whose interior is decorated in baroque, rococo, and neoclassical styles. Amid the 10 acres of stunning gardens, fountains, and trails of this exquisite Italianate estate – the winter home of late farm-equipment magnate, James Deering – you'll find a gazebo and a stone gondola breakwater that look over Biscayne Bay.

The Barnacle (43)
3485 Main Hwy, Coconut Grove, FL 33133
☎ **(305) 448-9445** ➔ **(305) 448-7484**

🔲 *Bus 22, 27, 42, 48* 🅿 for the disabled 🕙 Fri.–Mon. 9am–4pm; Tue.–Thu. guided visits for groups only; closed Christmas and New Year ● $1 🔲 🔲 10am, 11.30am, 1pm, 2.30pm, English, French and Spanish 🔲 no upstairs

Anyone interested in the history of greater Miami should be sure to visit The Barnacle, the former home of naval architect Ralph Middleton Munroe. The two-story cracker-style house is a taste of old Miami. Its barnacle-shaped shaped roof protects true period furniture and vintage photographs. It sits upon five peaceful acres of hammock and waterfront, in the middle of bustling Coconut Grove. State employees share a wealth of information with visitors.

Not forgetting

■ **Museum of Science and Space Transit Planetarium (44)** 3280 S Miami Ave, Miami, FL 33129 ☎ (305) 854-4247 (museum) ; (305) 854-4242 (planetarium) 🕙 Mon.–Sun. 10am–6pm; closed Thanksgiving and Christmas; laser shows at Planetarium: Fri., Sat. 9pm, 10pm, 11pm and midnight ● $9 adults; $7 over-62s and students; $5.50 for 3-12years *With more than 140 hands-on exhibits, laser lights shows set to rock music, and intriguing tours of the stars, the museum and planetarium is a fun diversion for the scientifically inquisitive (especially the young and curious).* ■ **Ermita de la Caridad (45)** 3609 S Miami Ave, Miami, FL 33133 ☎ (305) 854-2404 🕙 Mon.–Sat. 9am–9pm; mass noon and 8pm *This conical church, built to face their homeland, has a place in the hearts of Cuban exiles. The gardens and fountain are built in part with pieces of the island itself.*

42

44

41

In the area
■▶ **Where to stay:** ➡ 32 ➡ 36
■▶ **Where to eat:** ➡ 40
■▶ **After dark:** ➡ 72 ➡ 74 ➡ 76
■▶ **Where to shop:** ➡ 122 ➡ 125 ➡ 130

What to see

Fairchild Tropical Garden (46)
10901 Old Cutler Road, Miami, FL 33156
☎ (305) 667-1651 ➡ 305-661-8953

🔲 65 🅿 🕐 *daily 9.30am–4.30pm; closed Dec 25* ● *$8; free 0–12 years* 🔲 🔳
by tram on the hour, 10am–4pm, on foot Nov.–Apr. Mon.–Fri. 10.30am, 11.30am;
Sat., Sun. 10.30am, 11.30am, 1.30pm 🔲 🔲 🔲 🔲

Tropical plants of all varieties populate the largest tropical botanical
garden in the U.S. A tram ride winds through 83 acres of ponds, palms, and
exotic foliage and fruits. Don't miss Cycad Circle, where you'll witness the
same flora that dinosaurs consumed more than 350 million years ago.
There are also fascinating lectures and events throughout the year.

Miami Metrozoo (47)
12400 SW 152nd Street, Miami, FL 33177
☎ (305) 251-0400 ➡ 305-378-6381

Ⓜ *Dadeland South and beyond* 🔲 *Coral Reef Max* 🅿 🕐 *9.30am–5.30pm*
(ticket office 9.30am–4pm) ● *$8; $4 3–12 years* 🔲 🔳 *by miniature train, times*
vary, English $2; ask for other languages 🔲 🔲 🔲

Be prepared to walk and walk and walk at this extensive animal
sanctuary. Exotic creatures from around the world stroll in open
habitats, not inside cages. The white Bengal tiger, gibbons, elephants, and
other creatures are so close you can see the expressions on their faces.
Lectures, demonstrations, and shows take place throughout the day.

Coral Castle (48)
28655 S Dixie Hwy, Homestead, FL 33030
☎ (305) 248-6345 ➡ (305) 248-6344

Ⓜ *Dadeland South and beyond* 🔲 *South Busway Max* 🅿 🕐 *Mon.–Thu.*
9am–6pm, Fri.–Sun. 9am–7pm ● *$7.75 adults; $6.50 over-62s; $5 7–12years*
🔲 🔳 *Fri.–Tue.* 🔲 🔲 *www.coralcastle.com*

If you've ever done anything crazy for love, it's likely to fall short of this
eerie site. Latvian immigrant Edward Leedskalnin single-handedly carved
and moved every object – including the goliath chairs, nine-ton gate, and
oversized telescope – in tribute to a sixteen-year-old girl who jilted him
back home.

Not forgetting

■ **Parrot Jungle (49)** 11000 SW 57th Ave, South Miami, FL 33156
☎ (305) 666-7834 🕐 *daily 9.30am–6pm* ● *$14.95 adults; $12.95 students and
senior citizens; $8.95 for 3-10 years. Lush tropical garden with more than 1,100
species of birds and 100 varieties of plants. Trained parrot shows throughout the
day are fun for all.* ■ **Weeks Air Museum (50)** 14710 SW 128th Street,
Miami, FL 33186 🕐 *daily 10am–5pm* ☎ (305) 233-5197 ●; *$6.95 over-65s; $5.95
4–12 years. Old airplanes for flying enthusiasts.* ■ **Fruit and Spice Park (51)**
24801 SW 187th Ave, Homestead, FL 33031 ☎ (305) 247-5727 🕐 *daily
10am–5pm* ● *$1 0–12 years. Fruit trees and exotic species with intoxicating
perfumes; taste the windfalls, but no picking.* ■ **The Charles Deering Estate
(52)** 🕐 16701 SW 72nd Ave, Miami, FL 33157 ☎ (305) 235-1668 *A park with
tropical plants and a Mediterranean-style palace belonging to Charles Deering, the
brother of the owner of Vizcaya.*

46

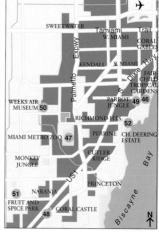

SWEETWATER

Tamiami Trail

W. MIAMI

CORAL GABLES

KENDALL   S. MIAMI

Palmetto Expwy

S. Dixie Hwy

FAIRCHILD TROPICAL GARDENS

WEEKS AIR MUSEUM **50**

PARROT JUNGLE **49** **46**

RICHMOND HTS.

52

MIAMI METRO ZOO **47**

PERRINE   CH. DEERING ESTATE

MONKEY JUNGLE

CUTLER RIDGE

US 1

PRINCETON

51   NARANJA

FRUIT AND SPICE PARK

48   CORAL CASTLE

Biscayne Bay

N

48

47

49

47

In the area

- **Where to stay:** ➡ 34
- **Where to eat:** ➡ 56 ➡ 58 ➡ 60
- **After dark:** ➡ 72
- **Where to shop:** ➡ 128

What to see

The Biltmore Hotel (53)

1200 Anastasia Ave, Coral Gables, FL 33134
☎ (305) 445-1926 ➡ (305) 913-3159

Ⓜ Metrorail Douglas Rd and beyond 🚌 Bus 72 Ⓟ 🅿 🕐 24hrs ● free 🗓 Sun.
1.30pm, 2.30pm, 3.30pm;Thu. 7pm stories about the Biltmore by the fireside 🏢
🍴 🍷 ♿ 📺 800-727-1926 @ www.biltmorehotel.com

Everything at the Biltmore, the jewel of Coral Gables, is a hymn to
sophistication: the 600,000-gallon swimming pool where Johnny
Weissmuller was a swimming instructor, the painted ceiling in the lobby,
the golf course... Within its Spanish style walls, Al Capone ran a
speakeasy, and celebrities such as Judy Garland, the Windsors, and the
Clintons engaged in private acts.

Venetian Pool (54)

2701 De Soto Blvd, Coral Gables, FL 33134 ☎ (305) 460-5356

🚌 Bus 24 Ⓟ 🕐 Tue.–Fri.: June–Aug. 11am–7.30pm; Sep., Oct. and Apr., May
11am–5.30pm; Nov.–Mar. 10am–4.30pm; Sat., Sun.: 10am–4.30pm ● Nov.–Mar.:
$5 adults; $2 3–12 years / Apr.–Oct.: $8 adults; $4 3–12 years; no children under
3 🍴 ♿ ♿

Built in 1923 from the remains of an old coral quarry, the pool served as a
set for Esther Williams and Johnny Weissmuller movies. Its arches,
waterfalls, caves, bridges, belvederes and loggias smothered in climbing
plants, give it a Venetian feel.

Coral Gables Merrick House (55)

907 Coral Way, Coral Gables, FL 33134
☎ (305) 460-5361

🚌 Bus 24 Ⓟ 🕐 Wed., Sun. 1pm–4pm or by appointment; closed public holidays ●
$2 adults; $0.50 children 🍴 🗓 English; Spanish and French occasionally ♿ 1st floor

The house of George Merrick, the founder of Coral Gables, contains many
family treasures, including artwork, photographs, family portraits and
personal items.

Not forgetting

■ **Lowe Art Museum (56)** 1301 Stanford Dr, Coral Gables, FL 33146
☎ (305) 284-3535 🕐 Tue.,Wed., Fri., Sat. 10am–5pm;Thu. noon–7pm; Sun.
noon–5pm ● $5 adults; $3 concessions . A strong collection spans Pre-Columbian
relics, paintings from El Greco and from Andy Warhol, and bright cloth from
Guatemala. ■ **Coral Gables City Hall (57)** 405 Biltmore Way, Coral
Gables, FL 33134 ☎ (305) 446-6800 🕐 Mon.–Fri. 8am–5pm inspired by the
Spanish Renaissance. ■ **Coral Gables Congregational Church (58)**
3010 De Soto Blvd, Coral Gables, FL 33134 ☎ (305) 448-7421 🕐 Mon.–Fri.
8.30am–4.30pm Raw cypress pews and cultural events. ■ **The
architectural styles of Coral Gables (59-62)**) When George Merrick
developed the city, he created villages of different architecture designed to capture
an 'old world' feeling. Four of the most significant are: a **Dutch South African
village (59)**, between 6612, 6700,6704 and 6710 SW 42nd Ave and 6705 San
Vicente St, a **Normandy village (60)**, between Vizcaya Ave, Alesio Ave,Vizcaya
Court, et SW 42nd Ave, a **Florida pioneer village (61)**, between 4320, 4409,
4515, and 4620 Santa Maria St, and a **Chinese village (62)**, between Sansovino
Ave, Castania Ave, Riviera Dr and Magiore St.

Most of the beaches in Miami were created only a few decades ago: mangroves had to be covered by tons of sand dredged up from the ocean. Occasionally, a hurricane hits the coast, destroying several yards of coastline. The dredgers then have to go back out to sea to collect piles of sand to tip on the beach.

What to see

Miami Beach (63-66)

🚌 *Bus C, G, H, L, M, S; Electrowave* 🅿️ *parking meters* 🕑 *dawn to dusk* ● *free*

In Miami each beach has its own personality and attracts its own followers. South Beach **(63)** extends from the far south of Miami Beach to 15th St. Lummus Park Beach, from 5th to 15th Street, is the beach for any self-respecting voyeur: row upon row of sculptured, bronzed bodies in tiny costumes. On the promenade girls and boys roller-blade up and down, old people play chess or dominos and others sit on the benches to chat or read... More sporty types play volleyball or test their fitness on the assault courses, while beyond the dunes you can lie in the sun, swim or play badminton. The beach has several observation posts for lifeguards. These distinctive wooden towers, painted in bright colors are reminiscent of 'Baywatch'. From 5th to 11th Streets mermaids bask in the sun (topless of course). Beyond that, to the north, is the start of the gay area. A wooden footbridge between 21st St. and the Eden Roc Hotel on 45th St. marks the Mid-Beach beaches **(64)**. Here, at any hour of the day, you will meet locals out for a walk or a jog. The beach alongside is usually less crowded than the others, except near the large hotels. The two beaches at North Beach **(65)** are ideal for escaping too many people. The Art-Deco buildings (sadly not yet restored) are worth a look. And for those wanting an all-over tan, Haulover Beach **(66)** at the north of Bal Harbor is the naturist beach.

Key Biscayne (67-70)

🚌 *Bus B* 🅿️ *parking meters* 🕑 *dawn to dusk* ● *free*

One of the rare beaches outside Miami Beach. Just beyond the toll booth for Rickenbacker Causeway, is Hoble Beach **(67)**, a spit of sand where windsurfers gather. Between the first and second bridge, on the left, is Virginia Beach **(68)**, which was, during segregation, the only beach open to African-Americans. Recently reopened, it is one of the most beautiful beaches in Miami. Crandon Park Beach **(69)**, a short distance past the second bridge, with barbecue grills, golf courses and soccer pitches is an ideal spot for an outdoor party. Surprisingly, the water there is the clearest in the city. Slightly further away, on the tip of Key Biscayne, is Bill Baggs Cape Florida State Recreation Area **(70)**, which boasts an ancient lighthouse.

Matheson Hammock Park (71)
9610 Old Cutler Road, Miami, FL 33156 ☎ (305) 445-5475

🚌 *65 (limited timetable)* 🅿️ *$3.50* 🕑 *Mon.–Fri. 8.30am–5pm; Sat., Sun. 8.30am–6pm* ● *free* 🍴 🌿 🚻 ♿

Here you can bathe in a natural atoll, surrounded by a beach planted with palm trees at the edge of Fairchild Tropical Garden. The racoons are very friendly (almost too friendly) and 'invite' visitors to share their meals with them.

71

64

64

66

65

64
MIAMI
BEACH

63

67

68 VIRGINIA
KEY

69
KEY
BISCAYNE

70

71

ATLANTIC
OCEAN

N

64

63

70

63

67

99

The 'river of grass'

Everglades National Park is home to the reserve of the Miccosukee, a Seminole tribe who took refuge in the area around 1850. The Miccosukee Indian Village is a sort of model village, situated by the Tamiami Trail (US 41). Here you can buy local crafts and taste traditional food such as alligator tail. You can also risk a ride on the Pa-hay-okee, the 'river of grass', on a fast airboat, driven by an Indian guide.

Miccosukee Indian Village
U.S. Highway 41, 20 20 miles east of Oasis Visitor Center
☎ *(305) 223-8380 Airboat rides :*
🕐 *9.30am–5pm ● $7for half an hour*

Fishing in The Keys

Keen fishermen from all over the world flock to the famous Florida Keys Fly Fishing School at Islamorada. You can pay to have the services of a guide for half a day or a full day. You can also have a weekend learning to fish.
Florida Keys Outfitters, *Mile Marker 82, Islamorada* ☎ *(305) 664-5423*

17
Days out

THE INSIDER'S FAVORITES

Day trips

Many tour operators offer day trips by coach to the Everglades, Fort Lauderdale, Key West, Sawgrass Mills Mall and other places in South Florida.
For information and reservations:
Flamingo Tours
17070 Collins Ave, Miami Beach
☎ *(305) 948-3822*
Miami Nice Tours
18090 Collins Ave, Suite T11,
Miami Beach
☎ *(305) 931-8058*

Boat trips

Many ships depart from Miami for short trips (3–4 days) to Key West and other islands in the Gulf of Mexico, as well as to the Caribbean. Prices range from $350 to $600 on Carnival, Norwegian and Royal Caribbean Cruise lines. There is no agency offering reduced fares.
Cruise Experts
1125 SW 87th Ave, Miami
☎ *(305) 264-3434*
🕙 *Mon.–Fri. 10am–5.30pm*
@ *www.cruisexperts.com*

Trips outside Miami should delight those who love white sand (Sanibel Island), wild, open spaces (Everglades), diving (The Keys) or just shopping... But do take an organized trip or rent a car, as public transport leaves a lot to be desired!

Further afield

Fort Lauderdale (1–4)
➡ 104

27 miles

🚌 Take the I-95 north to the Fort Lauderdale exit; for Sawgrass Mills Mall, take the Florida Turnpike north to Sunrise Boulevard, take the Boulevard west and continue as far as Flamingo Road (about 45 mins for Fort Lauderdale; about 55 mins for Sawgrass Mills Mall).

Palm Beach County (5–8)
➡ 104

67 miles (West Palm Beach)

🚌 For Palm Beach take the I-95 north to the Palm Beach, Belvedere Road or Okeechobee Boulevard exits, take the eastbound exit and cross the bridge over the Intracoastal Waterway; for Palm Beach Polo and Country Club, take the I-95 north to Forest Hills Boulevard, take the Boulevard westbound and continue for 10 miles to Polo Club Road; for Morikami Museum and Japanese Gardens, take the I-95 north to Yamato Road (exit 40 West), take Yamato Road west and continue for 4 miles to Jog Road, turn right and continue for 3 miles to Morikami Park Road (about 90 mins either destination).

Naples (9)
➡ 108

125 miles

🚌 Take the I-95 north to the 595, continue west to the I-75, then west again on the I-75 to Naples (about 2 hrs 30 mins).

Fort Myers (10)
➡ 108

143 miles

🚌 Take the I-95 north to the 595, then west to the I-75; on the I-75, exit at junction 23, then continue on the FLA

82 (Dr Martin Luther King Jnr Boulevard) which becomes McGregor Boulevard (about 3 hrs).

Sanibel Island (11)
➡ 108

158 miles
 Take the I-95 north to the 595, then west to the I-75; continue on the I-75 north to Daniels Parkway which you take westbound; turn left into Summerlin

Road (869) and continue along Sanibel Causeway (about 3 hrs).

Florida Keys (12–15)
➡ 110
Key West: 161 miles

 Take Florida Turnpike south to the US1 (Overseas Highway), then continue southwards. (From Miami International Airport: 1hr 30 mins to John Pennecamp Coral Reef State Park, 2 hrs 30 mins to the Dolphin Research Center, 3 hrs to Bahia Honda State Recreation Area, 4 hrs for Key West).

Everglades (16–17)
➡ 112
Shark Valley entrance: 25 miles; Everglades City 65 miles
 Main entrance S.R. 836 westbound to Florida Turnpike, then take the Turnpike south to Florida City, turn right and follow the signs on the S.R. 9336 (1 hr 15mins).
Shark Valley entrance: S.R. 836 west to Florida Turnpike, take the Turnpike south, leave on the Tamiami Trail (US 41) and continue 30 miles westbound (45 mins).
Everglades City : take the I-75 or the US 41westbound to the S.R.29, then south to Everglades City (about 1 hr 30 mins).

Whether for its vast sandy beaches, its canals bordered by villas and luxurious gardens or its first-class cultural events, Fort Lauderdale is a favorite spot for all types of family holiday. But the county of Broward, of which Fort Lauderdale is the capital, also attracts keen shoppers who like to stroll along Las Olas Boulevard or around the huge shopping

Further afield

Beachfront (1)

on the Interstate A1A, 2 miles between SE 17th Street and Sunrise Blvd, Fort Lauderdale, FL 33316

P **🕐** *open 24 hrs* ● *free*

For a long time Fort Lauderdale beach was a favorite for students who transformed it into a massive nightclub during the spring vacation. At the beginning of the 1990s, the town evicted these rowdy merry-makers and invested $26 million in revamping the whole coastal area. Now the vast beaches studded with palm trees and parasols are besieged by well-off tourists and families playing volleyball and diving. Wide paths between the road and the beach give you the chance to walk or roller-blade in peace, and cafés, restaurants and souvenir shops have taken over the seafront.

Museum of Discovery & Science and Blockbuster IMAX Theater (2)

401 S W 2nd St, Fort Lauderdale, FL 33312
☎ (954) 467-6637 o (954) 463-IMAX

🕐 *Mon.–Sat. 10am–5pm, Sun. noon–6pm* ● ***Museum**: $8 adults, $5 children, $6 senior citizens **IMAX** $9 adults; $8 senior citizens; $7 children; double tickets: $12.50 adults; $11.50 senior citizens; $10.50 children* **▭** **🎟** **🍴** *Subways and Steve's, 10am–7pm*

Children will love this museum which celebrates the wonders of science and technology. Visitors are greeted by the Great Gravity Clock, the largest kinetic energy sculpture in Florida, then there are some 200 interactive displays to try out inside. An IMAX theater, with a giant screen and one of the most sophisticated sound systems in the world, offers a huge variety of movies, some in 3-D.

Las Olas Boulevard (3)

This elegant boulevard with its distinctive wooden houses is the nerve center of Downtown. There are almost two and a half miles of boutiques, art galleries, jewelers' shops and some of the best restaurants and nightclubs. Take a horse-drawn carriage in the evening and soak in the atmosphere. Nearby, at 335 SE 6th Ave, is **Stranahan House**, the oldest house in Fort Lauderdale (1901). At no. 1 East Las Olas Boulevard is the **Museum of Art**, a 1958 building devoted to contemporary art, showing prestigious works of art, including some by Andy Warhol.

Sawgrass Mills Mall (4)

12801 W Sunrise Blvd, at junction with Flamingo Road, Sunrise, Ft Lauderdale, FL 33323 **📞** 800 FL-MILLS

🚌 *Shuttle from Miami Beach hotels* **P** **🕐** *Mon.–Sat. 10am–9.30pm; Sun. 11am–8pm* **▭** **🚌** **🍴** **♿**

Just to the west of Fort Lauderdale, this is the largest shopping center in the world, offering huge discounts. More than 300 brands on one site, plus a Psychic Fair, for things paranormal and the occult. Wear comfortable shoes: the shops, restaurants, cinemas and other leisure activities are spread over 8 acres.

center of
Sawgrass Mills
Mall.

Designed by
Arquitectonica,
Sawgrass Mills is
more than a shopping
center: it is a real
tourist attraction!

1

2

3

To the north of Miami, the long, narrow island of Palm Beach has retained the rather posh atmosphere of the late 19th century, when it was the vacation resort favored by the American elite. Here, for over a century, celebrities and rich and influential families such as the Rockefellers, Pulitzers and Kennedys have been building sumptuous villas, surrounded by grand

 # Further afield

Morikami Museum and Japanese Gardens (5)
4000 Morikami Park Rd, Delray Beach, FL 33446 ☎ (561) 495-0233

P **☉** *Park* from dawn to dusk; *Museum* Tue.–Sun.10am–5pm; *Tea ceremony* 3rd Sat. of the month noon, 1pm, 2pm, 3pm ● *Park* free; *Museum* $5.25 adults; $4.75 senior citizens; $3 6–18 years *Tea ceremony* $3 ▒ Cornell Café, Tue.–Sun.11am–3pm

Just before Palm Beach. A rather unexpected place to find a Japanese garden! In 1905 Japanese pioneers founded an agricultural community to grow rice and tea, but it closed in 1920. Today the villa is home to a museum devoted to Japanese culture. You can stroll along leafy paths, between waterfalls and ponds of wriggling carp, meditate in the Zen garden and admire the bonsai trees... On the third Saturday of each month traditional tea ceremonies are held every hour from noon to 3pm.

Worth Avenue (6)
Palm Beach, FL 33480

The most prestigious labels (Cartier, Armani, Vuitton...) vie with each other for chic along this avenue lined with elegant palm trees and Spanish-style buildings designed by Addison Mizner. For the chosen few!

The Henry Morrison Flagler Museum (7)
1 Whitehall Way, Palm Beach, FL 33480 ☎ (561) 655-2833

P **☉** Tue.–Sat. 10am–5pm; Sun. noon–5pm ● $8 adults; $3 under–12s ▒ ▒ ▒

A sign of the American golden age, this palace built in the early 20th century for Henry Flagler (1830-1913) contains no fewer than 55 rooms. The mansion, nicknamed the 'Taj Mahal' of America, is now listed in the National Register of Historical Monuments and has been turned into a museum. Its beauty rivals that of the luxurious villas of Newport, Rhode Island: precious marble, gilding, majestic staircases and murals by Louis Comfort Tiffany. Do not miss the Louis XIV music room and the Louis XV ballroom.

Palm Beach Polo and Country Club (8)
11809 Polo Club Rd, West Palm Beach, FL 33414 ☎ (561) 793-1440

P **☉** Jan.–Apr. Sun. 3pm ● free entry; seats $11-40, free for under-12s ▒ Polo Café ♫

One of the largest polo grounds in the world. Sacrifice a few dollars to get a seat so you can admire celebrities and heiresses from close up; the entertainment is to be found on the terraces as well as on the field!

Not forgetting
■ **Taboo** 221 Worth Ave, Palm Beach, FL 33480 ☎ (561) 835-3500 ●●● *American Bistro. For when you are shopping on Worth Avenue.*
■ **The Breakers Hotel** 1 S County Rd, Palm Beach, FL 33480
▼ 800-833-3141 ●●●●● *Historical hotel in Palm Beach decorated by European artists.*

parks, as their winter residences. Palm Beach is without a doubt the symbol of the American dream.

After the lively nightlife of Miami, pause for a while on Florida's unspoilt southwest coast. A chance to take a step back in time in Naples, to relax on one of the fabulous white sand beaches on the mainland or on Sanibel Island, or to explore the extraordinary nature reserves. Everywhere you will find viewpoints from which you will be able to

Further afield

Naples (9)

Naples is an elegant seaside town whose ambition is to become the international golf capital. In 'Olde Naples', the city center, are charming tree-lined streets, Victorian villas, beautiful shops, galleries and restaurants (Third Street South). From Naples Pier, built to replace the first one (1888), is a wonderful view of the villas on Millionaires' Row – or you can admire the unbelievable sunset.

Fort Myers (10)

Edison and Ford Winter Estates, 2350 McGregor Blvd, Fort Myers, FL 33901 ☎ (941) 334-3614 🅿 ☑ *Mon.–Sat. 9am–3.30pm; Sun. noon–3.30pm* ● *adult couple's ticket $11; $5.50 for 6–12 years* ▢ ▢

Thomas Alva Edison (1847-1931) moved to Fort Myers in 1885 to complete his research into the electric lamp filament. You can visit the house, the botanical garden, with some 6,000 species, and the laboratory where he perfected the phonograph, the kinetoscope (forerunner of the cinematograph) and the teleprinter. The adjacent villa, Mangoes, was the winter residence of the car manufacturer Henry Ford (1863-1947), a good friend of Edison.

Sanibel Island (11)

🅿 *toll Sanibel Causeway: $3 return; parking meters on beach front 1 hr $0.75 JN "Ding" Darling National Wildlife Refuge*, 1 Wildlife Dr, Sanibel Island, FL 33957 ☎ (941) 472-1100 *Visitor Center* ☑ *Nov.–Apr.: daily 9am–5pm. May–Oct. Mon.–Thu., Sat. 9am–4pm; "Wildlife Drive"* ☑ *Sat.–Thu. dawn to dusk* ● *$5 per car $1 per pedestrian or cyclist; miniature train ride: $8 adults, $4 concessions Bailey-Matthews Shell Museum*, 3075 Sanibel-Captiva Rd, Sanibel Island, FL 33957 ☎ (941) 395-2233 ☑ *Tue.–Sun. 10am–4pm* ● *$5 adults $3 8–16 years* ▦

The Lee County Barrier Islands off Fort Myers form a sort of low broken ridge in the Gulf of Mexico. The largest, Sanibel Island, has beach after beach of white sand literally strewn with shells (collecting is forbidden!) and is dotted with sumptuous villas, lush natural parks and nature reserves. At the extreme southwest of the island is a lighthouse built in 1884 from which it is possible to see Naples. The biggest attraction on Sanibel Island is the **JN "Ding" Darling National Wildlife** refuge in the north – almost 5,000 acres of mangrove swamp crossed by a maze of canals. You can follow the spectacular 'Wildlife Drive' across the reserve by car, bicycle or on foot, or by joining an organized trip by miniature train or canoe: a chance to see alligators, otters, racoons, spoonbills, egrets and herons close up. **The Bailey-Matthews Museum** is unique in the United States and houses more than a million shells from all over the world and a collection of 'Valentines', shell boxes made by the indigenous population of Barbados.

Not forgetting

■ **McT's Shrimphouse & Tavern** 1523 Periwinkle Way, Sanibel Island, FL 33957 ☎ (941) 472-3161 ●● *Fish.*
■ **The Dock at Crayton Cove** 812 12th Ave South, Naples ☎ (941) 263-9940 ●● *Eclectic cuisine, and a view over the bay.*

admire the beautiful sunsets surrounded by a 'green glow'.

9

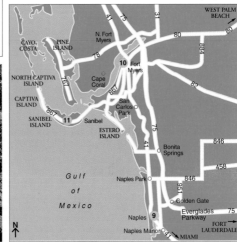

11

11

11

11

The southern tip of Florida is a long string of small coral islands stretching 200 miles from Biscayne Bay to Key West and the Dry Tortugas, which are only 90 miles from Cuba. The forty-three bridges of the 'Freeway over the sea' link them in an endless chain and give the impression of floating on the water. The Keys are a paradise for diving

Further afield

John Pennekamp Coral Reef State Park (12)
US 1, Mile Marker 102.5, Key Largo, FL 33037 ☎ (305) 451-1202

🅘 *Mon.–Sun. 8am–sunset* ● *$4 per car plus $1.00 per person, $1.00 per pedestrian or cyclist* 🔲 🔳 🔳 🔳 🔳

This aquatic park covering an area of over 115 square miles protects the only living coral reef in mainland United States, and is host to many varieties of coral and fish. You can rent diving equipment (mask and snorkel), visit the coral reefs by glass-bottomed boat or explore the footpaths through the mangroves and wild tamarind trees.

Dolphin Research Center (13)
US 1, Mile Marker 59, Marathon, FL 33050 ☎ (305) 289-1121

🅿 🅘 *9am–4pm* ● *12.50 adults; $10 senior citizens; $7 4–12 years; reservations necessary (before the first of the month for the following month): 'Dolphin Encounter' $110 per person; Dolphin Splash (in the water, not swimming) $60 per person* 🔲 🔳 *educational trips on foot 10am, 11am, 12.30pm, 2pm, 3.30pm* 🔳

This educational and research institute is famous throughout the United States; you can swim and play with a family of fifteen Atlantic dolphins under the supervision of an experienced guide. If you have not booked in advance, it is still worth asking – there may be a place free on the Dolphin Splash program!

Bahia Honda State Recreation Area (14)
US 1, Mile Marker 37, Big Pine Key, FL 33043 ☎ (305) 872-2353

🅿 🅘 *8am–sunset* ● *$4 per car plus $1.00 per person, $1.00 per pedestrian or cyclist, free under 5 years* 🔳

A park created on one of the most beautiful coasts of South Florida where you can swim, fish, walk or just look at the birds in their differing ecosystems: beaches of white sand, mangroves, lagoons and tropical undergrowth, and the deep water is just perfect for diving into.

Key West (15)

🅿 *Ernest Hemingway Home and Museum, 907 Whitehead St, Key West, FL 33040 ☎ (305) 294-1575* 🅘 *9am–5pm* ●*$8 adults; $5 6–12 years* 🔲 🔳

Situated at the 'end of the road', nearer to Cuba than to Miami, Key West has retained a colonial atmosphere and its own distinctive character. Everyone meets up in Mallory Square for the sunset ceremony in the evenings; music is in full swing, acrobats and other street entertainers bring the area to life. Reminders of Hemingway are never far away in Key West; he wrote several of his books here, including To Have and Have Not. Even if he did not live on the island permanently, he bought a Spanish colonial house in 1931, which is now a museum.

Not forgetting

■ **Blue Heaven** 729 Thomas St, Key West, FL 33040 ☎ (305) 296-8666 ●● *An old brothel, where Hemingway attended cock fights. The restaurant serves excellent Caribbean food, mainly fish.*

and deep-sea fishing, but they also attract those of a romantic nature with their legendary sunrises and sunsets over the Atlantic and the Gulf of Mexico.

12

13

14

15

Everglades National Park is the only American park to be designated a World Heritage Site by UNESCO because of its International Biosphere Reserves. The Seminole Indians gave the immense marshland its nickname, 'river of grass', because of its vegetation. The park boasts exceptional flora and fauna, including some endangered species.

Further afield

Everglades National Park (16)
35 miles south-west of Miami ☎ (305) 242-7700

🕐 *daily, depending on the water level.* **Main entrance** 🕐 *24 hours* ● *$10 per car and trailer, $5 per cyclist or pedestrian (tickets valid 7 days).* **Tourist Information: Ernest F. Coe Visitor Center** ☎ *(305) 242-7700* 🕐 *8am–5pm* ● *free entry to Visitor Center* ▣ 🚻 🏢 **Entrance, Shark Valley** *Tamiami Trail (US41) 35 miles west of Miami* 🕐 *8.30am–6pm* ● *$8 per car and trailer, $4 per cyclist or pedestrian (valid 7 days).* **Tourist Information: Shark Valley Visitor Center** ☎ *(305) 221-8776* 🕐 *8.30am–5pm Guided tours by miniature train* ☎ *(305) 221-8455* 🕐 *Nov.–Apr. 9am–4pm $8 adults; $7 senior citizens; $4 under-12s* ▣ 🚻

Most of the southern tip of Florida is taken up by the Everglades, a vast swampy area crossed by a long watercourse which flows very slowly from Lake Okeechobee toward Florida Bay. Everglades National Park was founded in 1947 to safeguard this fragile ecosystem, the only one of its kind in the world. The park is home to several endangered species, such as the Florida panther, the American crocodile, the southern bald eagle and the West Indian manatee as well as alligators, racoons, sea turtles, 300 varieties of birds (ibis, pelicans, flamingos, spoonbills...) and a myriad of insects including 'ferocious' mosquitos! It is also very rich in flora, including twenty-five species of orchid. There are several points of entry; the main entrance is the east side of the park. The well-equipped Ernest Coe Visitors Information Center has details on the best walking and canoe trails, campsites and observation posts. Flamingo Lodge, Marina and Outpost Resort offer guided tours by 'airboat' (a flat-bottomed boat which is moved over the surface of the 'river of grass' by an airplane propeller) and rents canoes, boats and cycles. Shark Valley, on the north side of the park, is ideal for bicycle rides and watching alligators... (safest from the top of a 15-yard-high viewing tower!). One further precaution is to time your visit for the dry season (end Nov.–Apr.) when temperatures and humidity are lower and there are fewer mosquitos.

Everglades City (17)

🕐 *Tourist Information: Gulf Coast Visitor Center, route SR 29* ☎ *(941) 695-3311* ● *free entry to the park; Smallwood's Store Museum, Mamie St., Everglades City, FL 34139* ☎ *(941) 695-2989*

This town situated near to the western entrance to the park was founded in the 1920s, but its commercial development was never as great as had been hoped. Nevertheless, it remains a good starting point to explore the Everglades by boat or canoe. Smallwood's Store Museum, which tells the story of the life of pioneers in the early 20th century, is worth a visit.

Not forgetting

■ **Flamingo Lodge** | Flamingo Lodge Hwy, Everglades National Park, Flamingo, FL 33034 ☎ (941) 695-3101 ●● ▣ 🏨 🍺 🏊 *103 rooms and 24 cottages with a view over Florida Bay* ■ **Flamingo Restaurant** | Flamingo Lodge Hwy, Everglades National Park, Flamingo, FL 33034 ☎ (941) 695-3101 ● 🕐 *Nov.–Apr. 7am–9pm. American and fish dishes.*

FORT
MYERS

PALM BEACH

NAPLES

75 Interstate Hwy.

SUNRISE

FORT
LAUDERDALE

BIG CYPRESS
NATIONAL
PRESERVE

NORTH MIAMI

MIAMI
BEACH

NAPLES

17

41 U.S. Hwy.

(Tamiami Trail)

MIAMI

Pinecrest

Shark
Valley

ATLANTIC
OCEAN

Gulf
of
Mexico

16

EVERGLADES

Homestead
Florida City

NATIONAL PARK

Visitor
Center

Flamingo

KEY WEST

N

Opening times

Unlike in Europe and Latin America, stores in Miami do not close for lunch. In most malls, they stay open until 9 or 9.30pm Monday to Saturday and until 6pm on Sundays. In the tourist areas many remain open past 11pm. In the downtown business areas, however, expect them to close shortly after the offices (between 5.30pm and 7pm).

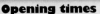

 # Where to shop

Watches and electronic goods

In the Downtown Business District, between Southeast 1st Street to Northwest 3rd Street, 2nd Avenue West and Biscayne Boulevard, you can buy computers, cameras and laptops, as well as watches and jewelry, all at discounts. Be prepared to bargain with the shopkeepers for the best prices.

Off to the shops!

To help tourists get to the big malls, most of which are situated outside the downtown areas, large hotels offer shuttle services. This is usually free, but it is customary to give a tip of $1 per passenger to the driver. Ask at your hotel.

Auctions and flea markets

Miamians are sentimental about 'old' things ... but here old might mean the sixties and seventies. There is plenty to be had, including bric-à-brac and antiques. Look in the classified section of *The Miami Herald* for times and venues of flea markets and auctions.

44 Stores

THE INSIDER'S FAVORITES

The Bank of America Coconut Grove Festival

In February, during President's Day weekend, more than three hundred artists from all over the United States gather in Coconut Grove (from 10am to 6pm) to exhibit and sell their works, making this one of the largest national art festivals. It has been going on for nearly four decades and always draws big crowds. The Bank of America will no longer be a sponsor after 2001.
For information phone ☎ (305) 447-0401 @ coconutgroveartsfest.com

Where to shop

Cynthia Rowley (1)
229 8th St., Miami Beach, FL 33139 ☎ (305) 674-8338 ➡ (305) 674-8969

🔲 H, C, K, Flagler Max; Electrowave **Women's fashions and accessories**
🕐 Mon.–Wed. 11am–7pm; Thu.–Sat. 11am–10pm; Sun. noon–6pm ▭ 🔳

Evening wear and accessories fill three display windows on 8th Street; shimmering materials and intoxicating femininity. Besides a resolutely elegant and slightly nostalgic collection with long, Hollywood-inspired dresses, this young American designer also offers a leather collection which is selling well and a smaller line featuring strong oriental influences. Shoes, bags, jewelry, glasses and cashmere shawls in earth tones.

Kenneth Cole (2)
190 8th Street Miami Beach, FL 33139
☎ 305-673-5151 ➡ 305-673-3848

🔲 H, C, K, Flagler Max; Electrowave **Fashion, shoes and accessories**
🕐 Mon.–Sat. 10am–10pm; Sun. 11am–8pm

Most known for his stylish and comfortable shoes, designer Kenneth Cole has expanded into a full line of clothing for men and women. Keeping up with the times, the South Beach store has followed suit and now offers sportswear that is perfect for South Beach clubbing as well as some more dressy elements at reasonable prices.

Urban Outfitters (3)
653 Collins Ave, Miami Beach, FL 33139
☎ (305) 535-9726 ➡ (305) 532-4573

🔲 H, C, K, Flagler Max; Electrowave **Fashion, accessories and bric-à-brac**
🕐 Mon.–Sat. 11am–10pm; Sun. noon–9pm ▭ @ www.urbn.com 🔵 Shops at Sunset Place, 5701 Sunset Dr, Miami, FL 33143 ☎ (305) 663-1536

A huge retail market on two floors. With up-to-the-minute fashions, including original and unusual outfits for young men and women. On the ground floor, home and gift items and women's apparel; on the second floor, books on intimate subjects, accessories and household goods: batik bedcovers, inflatable seats, multicolored cushions and some small objects such as frames and candles.

Not forgetting
■ **Natural Food Market (4)** 1011 5th St, Miami Beach, FL 33139 ☎ (305) 535-9050 Organic products, natural foods, vitamins, macrobiotic and vegetarian take-out meals and herbal medicines.
■ **A | X Armani Exchange (5)** 760 Collins Ave, Miami Beach, FL 33139 ☎ (305) 531-5900 Designed with the American market in mind, this line is more casual than most Armani collections. Affordable prices. Accessories.
■ **Versace Jeans Couture (6)** 755 Washington Ave, Miami Beach, FL 33139 ☎ (305) 532-5993 A black wrought-iron gate at the entrance to a stone arcade bearing Gianni Versace's symbol of two medusas, marks the entrance to the only shop opened by the designer himself, in South Beach. Jeans Couture is the latest and cheapest Versace line – made with the nocturnal creatures of South Miami Beach in mind.

Miami has become one of the fashion capitals of the world, so all the major fashion houses have branches here.

Where to shop

Lincoln Road Markets (7)

Lincoln Rd, between Washington Ave and Alton Rd
☎ (305) 673-4991

▣ *A, C, G, H, K, L, M, R, S; Electrowave* **Markets** 🕐 **Antiques and Collectibles Market** *Oct.–May every other Sun. 9am–5pm;* **Farmers' Market** *Sun. 9am–5pm;* **Arts on the Road** *☎ (305) 672-ARTS, 2nd Tue. of the month* ☐ *(usually)*

Lincoln Road, one of the main drags through SoBe (the other is Ocean Drive), is a popular pedestrian mall dotted with mosaic fountains and bordered by a host of shops and restaurants. Every Sunday the market selling fruit and flowers, regional products and specialties makes it a riot of color. Every other week from October to May, there is also a collectors' market. And on the second Tuesday of the month 'The Arts on the Road' comes to the area to sell works of art.

Art Center South Florida (8)

800 and 924 Lincoln Rd, Miami, FL 33139
☎ (305) 674-8278 ➡ (305) 674-8772

▣ *A, G, L, M, R, S; Electrowave* **Art gallery** 🕐 *Wed.–Sun. 1pm–11pm* ☐

About a hundred aspiring artists work here. They take turns using this prime gallery space on Lincoln Road to display their work to the public.

Histoires de Parfums (9)

531 Lincoln Rd, Miami Beach, FL 33139
☎ (305) 534-7500 ➡ (305) 534-7530

▣ *A, C, G, H, K, L, M, R, S; Electrowave* **Perfumes** 🕐 *Mon.–Sat. 10am–11pm; Sun. 10am–10pm* ☐

One corner of the shop is devoted to the history of perfume from the 18th century to the present day. Antique bottles, copper stills, an 18th-century bath. This enchanting location invites you to take a trip through the world of perfumes. There are products for the body (including wonderful soaps) and the home (candles, pot-pourri) as well as unique perfumes sold in Retro-style bottles with metal stoppers representing the store's logo, the hot air balloon.

Not forgetting

■ **The 24 Collection (10)** 744 Lincoln Rd, Miami Beach, FL 33139 ☎ (305) 673-2455 *Antique chess-boards, collectors' glasses, unusual jewelry, funky items of clothing, primitive weapons.*
■ **Condal & Peñamil House (11)** 741 Lincoln Rd, Miami Beach, FL 33139 ☎ (305) 673-3194 *Have a drink and a hand-rolled cigar in this wood-floored house. The ritual starts every evening at 7pm.*
■ **Senzatempo (12)** 1655 Meridian Ave, Miami Beach, FL 33139 ☎ (305) 534-5588 *Furniture, sculptures, jewelry, American and European bric-à-brac from the 1920s to the 1970s.*
■ **Española Way Market (13)** 15th St, Miami Beach, FL *A small, esoteric market held on Saturday and Sunday as part of the weekly Española Way sidewalk festival. You can find perfumed candles, kites, fresh flowers, organic products, amulets, stones and saris. You can have your palm read, enjoy a massage and have a tattoo or a henna design. Lots of fun. Bargains abound as the sun sets.*
■ **The 9th Chakra (14)** 811 Lincoln Rd, Miami Beach, FL 33139 ☎ (305) 538-0671 *All you need for Feng-Shui. Books, crystals, incense...*

Lincoln Road became known as Lincoln Mall since cars are not permitted and baby strollers can weave in and out of the many shops and restaurants.

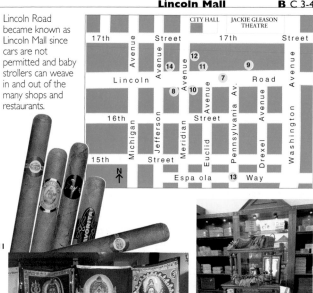

9

12

10

In the area
 Where to stay: ➥ 28
 Where to eat: ➥ 49 ➥ 60
 After dark: ➥ 72 ➥ 74
 What to see: ➥ 90 ➥ 98

Where to shop

Neiman Marcus (15)
9700 Collins Ave, Bal Harbour, FL 33154
☎ (305) 865-6161 ➥ (305) 864-7189

Bus G, H, K, S, T 🅿 *Department store* Mon.–Fri. 10am–9pm; Sat.
10am–7pm; Sun. noon–7pm International shipment Zodiac Mon.–Fri.
10am–8pm; Sat. 10am–5pm; Sun. noon–5pm 1-888-884-6136

A very select department store, like all Bal Harbour Shops: they are to
Miami what 5th Avenue is to New York, Bond Street is to London or Rue
du Faubourg St-Honoré is to Paris. This store only stocks the most
prestigious brands and luxury items. On the first floor are shoes,
perfumes, make-up, handbags and other accessories; on the second floor
big names in international fashion, and on the third lingerie, household
goods and linens such as tablecloths from Flanders and a delightful
restaurant.

Tartine et chocolat (16)
9700 Collins Ave, Bal Harbour, FL 33154
☎ (305) 861-1966 ➥ (305) 861-1229

Bus G, H, K, S, T 🅿 *Children's fashions* Mon.–Fri. 10am–9pm; Sat.
10am–7pm; Sun. noon–6pm

The absolutely precious French clothing here is made for the type of
children who never dig in the sandbox or play in the garden: cotton
piqué dresses with smocked bodices and wide, frilled skirts, or fancy,
striped suits with white trim. Children's bedding sets, teddy bears.

Tiffany & Co (17)
9700 Collins Ave, Bal Harbour, FL 33154
☎ (305) 864-1801 ➥ (305) 864-6549

Bus G, H, K, S, T 🅿 *Jewelry* Mon.–Wed. 10am–7pm; Thu. 10am–9pm; Fri.
10am–7pm; Sat. 10am–6pm; Sun. noon–6pm @ www.tiffany.com

Tiffany, the famous jewelry store, which inspired the equally famous film
starring Audrey Hepburn... Of course, that was the New York store. But
the Miami version is no less elegant, and Tiffany is still Tiffany. The
atmosphere is refined, the staff impeccable. This store is set in the
middle of a superb tropical garden and the big name will only allow
equally famous brands alongside it: Hermès, Versace, Prada, Dior...
Silverware, watches and jewelry by designers such as Paloma Picasso.

Oxygene (18)
9700 Collins Ave, Bal Harbour, FL 33154
☎ (305) 864-0202 ➥ (305) 861-4977

Bus G, H, K, S, T 🅿 *Ready-to-wear clothes* Mon.–Fri. 10am–9.30pm;
Sat. 10am–7pm; Sun. noon–6.30pm

Italian designers (Moschino, D & G, Blumarine, Ferretti) and an explosion
of colors in a rather surreal atmosphere with an extraordinary mixture
of styles – red velvet curtains and gilt mirrors and mosaics. A wide range
of day and evening wear. The long dresses, like the store, are rather
Baroque in style.

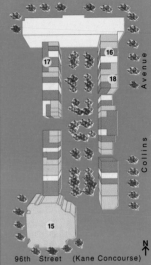

96th   Street   (Kane Concourse)

Harbour Shops is the most luxurious shopping mall in Miami; not surprisingly, all the big international designers have a presence there.

Vast shopping malls with large parking garages usually contain several department stores and a good many smaller specialty stores. Usually well air-conditioned, they have a bright, comfortable ambience with benches, restrooms, restaurants and cafés scattered throughout the malls, so you can take a break from your hectic shopping schedule!

Where to shop

Dadeland Mall (19)
7535 N Kendall Dr, Miami, FL 33156
☎ (305) 665-6226 ➠ (305) 665-5012

M Metrorail Dadeland N 🚌 87, 88, 104 P *Shopping mall* 🕐 *Mon.–Sat. 10am–9.30pm; Sun. noon–7pm* ☐ *International shipment* 🏮 🍸 💻 ♿

As many as 170 specialty shops are to be found alongside Florida style **Burdines** (☎ 305/662-3311), with its typical palm-tree pillars and ceilings painted with skies. One wing contains furniture, carpets, kitchen utensils and crystal, the other clothing and perfumes. For clothing and accessories from Chanel, Gucci and Fendi, pay a visit to the sophisticated and pricey **Saks Fifth Avenue** (☎ 305/662-8655). For casual clothes, shoes, and household goods try **Lord and Taylor** (☎ 305/284-8092); prices are reasonable, as they are at **JC Penney** (☎ 305/666-1911). After a break at **Starbucks Café**, explore **The Limited/Express/ Structure/Limited Too** (☎ 305/667-2405) – casual wear for men, women and children. Then rummage through the sale goods at **Cache** (☎ 305/667-5648), **Ann Taylor** (☎ 305/662-6612) or **Exit Shops** (☎ 305/667-1545). After that, cast an eye over **The Museum Company** (☎ 305/665-6077), which is packed with curious objects and scientific gadgets, and over **Radio Shack** (☎ 305/666-3296), a good place for electronic equipment. In neighboring Dadeland Station, do not forget the **Target** (☎ 305/668-0262) department stores. For cameras, hi-fi, telephones and computers, don't miss **Best Buy** (☎ 305/662-7073); for sports equipment and clothing, try **The Sports Authority** (☎ 305/667-2280).

The Falls (20)
8888 SW 136th St, Miami, FL 33176 ☎ (305) 255-4570 ➠ (305) 235-7248

🚌 *Bus 1, 52, Florida City Max, Coral Reef Max, Saga Bay Max, 231 Local* P *Shopping Mall* 🕐 *Mon.–Sat. 10am–9.30pm; Sun. noon–7pm* ☐ *International shipment* 🏮 🍸 💻 ♿ @ *www. thefallsshoppingcenter.com*

The prettily decorated, cool arcades, lush, tropical vegetation, fountains and ponds linked by bridges make you forget the hustle and bustle of the big city. Yet you can find anything here. Sandwiched between **Bloomingdales** (☎ 305/252-6300), a luxury fashion store renowned for its excellent service in ten languages, and **Macy's** (☎ 305/278-3282) are almost a hundred specialty stores. Have a look through **Pottery Barn** (☎ 305/238-0331) for decorative goods or in **Williams-Sonoma** (☎ 305/256-9929) for kitchen utensils fit for the best chefs. For lunch, try the Argentinian cuisine at **Los Ranchos**, or the hamburgers at **Johnny Rockets**.

Not forgetting

■ **Miami International Mall (21)** 1455 NW 107th Ave, Miami, FL 33172 ☎ (305) 593-1775 🕐 *Mon.–Sat.10am–9pm; Sun. 11am–6pm. A meeting of Europe and the Americas.* ■ **The Mall of the Americas (22)** 7795 W Flagler St, Miami, FL 33144 ☎ (305) 261-8772 🕐 *Mon.–Sat. 10am–9pm; Sun. noon–6pm. More Latin in character. Over one hundred specialty stores and a multiscreen cinema.*

Contrary to what you might expect, prices are not exorbitant in malls; never a day passes without some enticing sale!

19

19

19

20

19

20

Shopping mixed with entertainment... In these large shopping malls, which feel more like leisure parks, the arcades, plazas, staircases and terraces house huge, state-of-the-art movie theaters, auditoriums, cafés or restaurants. Will keep you occupied all day whether you are 7 or 77.

Where to shop

Aventura Mall (23)
19501 Biscayne Blvd, Aventura, FL 33180
☎ (305) 935-1110 ➠ (305) 935-4185

Bus 3 ☐P☐ *Shopping and entertainment mall* ☐ *Mon.–Sat. 10am–9.30pm; Sun. noon–8pm* ☐ *International shipment* ☐☐☐☐

Aventura Mall, recently revamped at a staggering cost, extends over several indoor areas, and some huge, bright, outdoor areas. **Burdines, Bloomingdale's, Macy's** (☎ 305/937-5485), **Lord & Taylor, JC Penney**: descriptions are unnecessary, such is their reputation. Outdoor enthusiasts will like **Sears** (☎ 305/937-7500) which favors American goods. Customers searching for original decorating ideas need look no further than **Restoration Hardware** (☎ 305/935-1253). When it comes to clothing, besides well-known brands of casual clothing, you can also find more unusual items such as the creations in bright tropical colors in **Mae** (☎ 305/936-9533) or the simple but elegant outfits of the French ready-to-wear house **Vertigo** (☎ 305/935-1050). Another store among the two hundred and fifty specialty shops deserving a particular mention, is **Build a Bear Workshop** (☎ 305/931-8676), where small, or even big children can make themselves a stuffed bear, cat, rabbit or some other animal of their choice. For a quick snack, try any of the kiosks at **Food Court**; for big portions of American **nouvelle cuisine**, the **Cheesecake Factory**; True gourmets will want to dine at **Paramount Grill** a more casual eatery by one of Miami's most famous Chef Allen; Perfect before or after a flick at the multiscreen movie theater with amphitheater-style seating. But entertainment is much in evidence in Aventura Mall – floorshows are often organized to keep shoppers amused.

The Shops at Sunset Place (24)
5701 Sunset Dr, Miami, FL 33143
☎ (305) 663-4222 ➡ (305) 663-0167

Ⓜ Metrorail South Miami Station 🚆 Bus 37, 48, 52, 57, 72 🅿 *Shopping and entertainment mall* 🕐 Mon.–Thu. 11am–10pm; Fri., Sat. 11am–11pm; Sun. 11am–9pm 📧 International shipment 🏧 📺 🖥 ♿ @ www.shopsimon.com

Among the newest of Miami's shopping malls, this sprawling complex has something for everyone. A huge twenty-four-screen movie theater and almost seventy stores, restaurants and cafés, interspersed with plazas and staircases, are hidden under the enormous porticos and artificial baobab trees. You could almost think you were in Disneyworld! The list of 'must do's' includes the **IMAX Theater**, whose six-story screen and state-of-the-art audio equipment allow films to be seen in 2- or 3-D (☎ 305/740-0399). And for video game fanatics of all ages, there is **Gameworks** (☎ 305/667-4263). The inevitable **Virgin Megastore** (☎ 305/665-4445)is there to keep the 'cultureholics' happy, with a range of CDs, books, videos and multimedia software big enough to satisfy even the most demanding. Those wanting to see life through rose-tinted glasses should go along to **Brookstone** (☎ 305/661-7175) full of amusing anti-stress gadgets. There is also a huge toy store for children, **FAO Schwarz**: (☎ 305/668-2300) collectors' Barbies, adorable cuddly toys and of course little Pokémons.

In the area
 Where to stay: ➡30
 Wheret to eat: ➡40 ➡50 ➡54
 After dark: ➡72 ➡76
 What to see: ➡88

➡ Where to shop

Bayside Marketplace (25)
401 Biscayne Blvd, Miami, FL 33132
☎ (305) 577-3344 ➡ (305) 577-0306

M *Metromover College/Bayside* **B** *Bus C, S, 3, 16, 95-Express, BISCAYNE MAX* **P** *charges* **Shopping and entertainment mall** ☉ *Mon.–Thu. 10am–10pm; Fri., Sat. 10am–11pm; Sun. 11am–9pm* ❑ � 🍴 🍸 🛍 🕭 🛒
@ *www.baysidemarketplace.com*

Adjacent to Bayfront Park, on Biscayne Boulevard, next to the brand new American Airlines Arena and to the Downtown Business District. One of its sections, Pier 5 Marketplace, celebrates the old Pier 5, on which Bayside was built. In the 40s and 50s this was one of the most popular tourist attractions in Miami, with its peculiar neon flying fish. Two floors where shops, storefronts, carts, and restaurants such as the Hard Rock Cafe are all blended together in a never ending festive atmosphere. Live Latin music, jazz, and blues compete with dance shows, mimes, and all sorts of open air performances. Perfect for shopping, fun, and relaxation in the glorious light and pleasant breeze of the bay. From T-shirts to authentic auto tags to the straw hats of **The Last Straw** (☎ 305/377-2711) to oriental objects in **A Passage to India** (☎ 305/375-9504), it is like being in a Latin-American bazaar. Then **The Disney Store** (☎ 305/371-7621) suddenly plunges you into the wonderful world of Mickey and Pluto. But you need to go on the **Warner Brothers Studio Store** (☎ 305/373-2312) to see the inimitable Sylvester and Tweety. A truly unique experience.

Seybold Building (26)
36 NE 1st St, Miami, FL 33132
☎ (305) 374-7922 ➡ (305) 374-5651

B *Bus 8, 9, 10, 11, 77* **P** *charges* **Jewelry center** ☉ *Mon.–Sat. 9am–6pm* ❑
@ *www.seyboldbldg.com*

The Seybold Building is not strictly speaking a shopping center; it is more a business center devoted to jewelry. Two hundred and eighty stores, both wholesale and retail, occupy the ten stories of the building. They say money does not smell, but even so there is an almost tangible atmosphere created by the billions of dollars which change hands here each day. Most customers are themselves jewelers coming to buy stones or gold, or have commissions or repairs carried out. Retail prices, however, remain reasonable. If you are looking for a precious stone or an original piece of jewelry, you are in the right place.

Not forgetting

■ **La Femme Lingerie (27)** 173 E Flagler St, Miami, FL 33132 ☎ (305) 372-1223 ☉ *Mon.–Sat. 9.30am–6.30pm. . Famous brands of lingerie, such as Victoria's Secret, Bali and Vanity Fair are sold here at half price.*

■ **Miami Golf Superstore (28)** 111 NE 1st St, 2nd story, Miami, FL 33132 ☎ (305) 371-4554 ☉ *Mon.–Fri. 9.30am–6pm; Sat. 10.30am–4.30pm. Huge and varied range of golfing accessories, all at very competitive prices.*

The Bayside Marketplace is like a huge bazaar, with its colored stalls and sideshows. It attracts increasing numbers of visitors into this waterfront area of Downtown, which is currently being refurbished.

In the area
▪ **Where to stay:** ➡ 34
▪ **Where to eat:** ➡ 56 ➡ 58 ➡ 60
▪ **After dark:** ➡ 72
▪ **What to see:** ➡ 96

Where to shop

GBS Beauty Supply (29)
308 Miracle Mile, Coral Gables, FL 33134
☎ (305) 446-6654 ➡ (305) 454-4928

▣ Bus J, 24, 40, 42, 52, 56, 72 🅿 *parking meters* **Cosmetics and beauty products** 🕐 *Mon.–Sat. 9am–6pm* ▭ @

Thousands of beauty and body-care products from all over the world: some brand names, but also some unusual or unique products. Everything can be viewed or tested. Most of the sales assistants are beauticians or hairdressers, who can offer their skills or simply advice.

Books and Books (30)
265 Aragon Ave, Coral Gables, FL 33134
☎ (305) 442-4408 ➡ (305) 444-9751

▣ Bus J, 24, 40, 42, 52, 56, 72 🅿 *parking meters* **Books** 🕐 *Mon.–Sat. 9am–11pm, Sun. 11am–8pm* ▭ @ *www.booksandbooks.com* ▮▮ *933 Lincoln Rd, Miami Beach, FL 33139 ☎ (305) 532-3222*

European-style bookstore with a huge range of art books, and frequent exhibitions by artists, photographers and writers. Here you will meet Miami's cultured classes as well as students from the neighboring university.

Scrivener's (31)
54 Miracle Mile, Coral Gables, FL 33134
☎ (305) 445-1003 ➡ (305) 445-0910

▣ Bus 24, 37 🅿 *parking meters* **Stationery** 🕐 *Mon.–Fri. 9am–6pm, Sat. 10am–3pm* ▭

The shop for those whose search for elegance extends to their writing materials: Mont-Blanc, Cartier, Dupont, Cross and Waterman plus other brands, as well as beautiful writing paper.

The House of Dolls (32)
86 Miracle Mile, Coral Gables, FL 33134
☎ (305) 648-1123 ➡ (305) 648-1125

▣ Bus 24, 37 🅿 **Dolls** 🕐 *Mon.–Sat. 10am–6pm* ▭ @ *www.houseofdolls.com*

A wonderful little shop, a kingdom of dolls: from floor to ceiling there are piles of Spanish dolls made of porcelain or paste-board (at exorbitant prices), and their little sisters, just as beautiful with their hand-made clothes, natural hair and leather ballet shoes (much more affordable). Impossible not to take one home.

Not forgetting

■ **Coral Gables Farmers' Market (33)** Merrick Park, 405 Biltmore Way, Coral Gables, FL 33134 ☎ (305) 460-5311 🕐 *Jan.–March: Sat. 8am–1pm Farmers and bakers offer their goods. Gardening lessons, cooking classes, and activities for the children sponsored by 'Books and Books'.*

■ **Barnes & Noble Booksellers (34)** 152 Miracle Mile, Coral Gables, FL 33134 ☎ (305) 446-4152 🕐 *Mon.–Sun. 9am–11pm A happy combination of bookstore and café.*

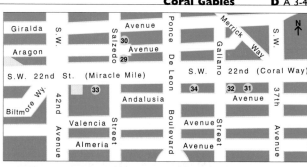

32

The relaxing atmosphere in Barnes & Noble encourages you to wander among the shelves where thousands of books just ask to be picked up and read...

31

30

34

For about ten years now, Miami has been a destination favored for shopping holidays, particularly by South Americans. Its network of shops tries to concentrate a huge range of specialty items in one place in an attempt to satisfy the needs and desires of its customers who are in a hurry to buy as much as possible before heading home.

Where to shop

CompUSA (35)
7440 N Kendall Dr, Miami, FL 33156
☎ (305) 670-5030 ➡ (305) 671-3098

M Metrorail Dadeland N ▦ Bus 87, 88, 104 P Computers ◑ Mon.–Sat. 9am–9pm; Sun. 10am–6pm ▬ 🔧 📺 1-800-266-7872 @ www.compusa.com
⬧ The Falls, 8851 SW 136th St, Miami, FL 33176-5816
☎ (305) 234-5600 ; 900 Park Centre Blvd #400, Miami, FL 33169
☎ (305) 620-1800

The Mecca for computer buffs. Compaq, Hewlett Packard, Apple, plus CompUSA products: computers, organizers, components, accessories, office and games software. Computers are sold ready to use, but you can also get them in kit form to build at home.

Wild Oats (36)
11701 S Dixie Hwy, Miami, FL 33157
☎ (305) 971-0900 ➡ (305) 971-0920

▦ Bus 52, Florida City Max, Coral Reef Max, Saga Bay Max, 231 Local P
Natural foods and vitamins ◑ Mon.–Sun. 8am–10pm ▬ 🍴 ▦ 🔧
@ www.wildoats.com ⬧ 1020 Alton Rd, Miami Beach, FL 33139 ☎ (305) 532-1707

Organic supermarket. Fruit and vegetables grown without fertilizers, meat from registered sources. Store suitable for vegetarians, vegans and others keen on healthy food. On the prepared meals counter can be found freshly prepared salads, spit-roast chickens and delicious bakery items. Perfect for a quick (and healthy) meal of above average quality.

Spy Tech International (37)
255 E Flagler St, Suite 84-85, Miami, FL 33131
☎ (305) 377-2156 ➡ (305) 377-2157

M Metromover Miami Avenue Station ▦ Bus C, K, S, 3, 16 P charges
Surveillance and self-defense items ◑ Mon.–Sat. 9.15am–6.30pm ▬
International shipment @ www.spytechinternational.com

The shop for the Inspector Gadget or James Bond lurking in all of us. Alarms and cameras of all descriptions, a wide range of equipment for investigations, surveillance and self-defense, plus specialty items as supplied to the police and the FBI! Some goods are illegal in the USA, and are available only for export.

Not forgetting
■ **Circuit City (38)** 7700 N Kendall Dr, Miami, FL 33156
☎ (305) 274-7733 Store specializing in electronics and household electronics. Look out for the weekly special offers on video cameras, walkie-talkies, laptops, computers, electronic organizers, digital cameras, etc.
■ **Miami Twice (39)** 6562 SW 40th Street, Miami, FL 33155 ☎ (305) 666-0127 Victorian clothing, accessories and other clothing, with lots of vintage stuff from the Sixties. Rental possible.
■ **Capt. Harry's Fishing Supplies (40)** 100 NE 11th St, Miami, FL 33132 ☎ (305) 374-4661 Wide range of fishing equipment and accessories for 'addicts' everywhere: Capt. Harry exports to over one hundred and sixty-two countries.

35

38

36

You want a rare bird? Purple leather high-tops? A Mardi Gras costume? Platform shoes? An outfit for a costume party? You are sure to find it in Greater Miami!

39

40

In the area

- **Where to stay:** ➥ 36
- **Where to eat:** ➥ 60 ➥ 62
- **After dark:** ➥ 72 ➥ 76
- **What to see:** ➥ 92

Where to shop

CocoWalk (41)
3015 Grand Ave, Coconut Grove, FL 33133
☎ (305) 444-0777 ➥ (305) 441-8936

🚌 Bus 6, 22, 27, 42, 48 🅿 charges **Shopping mall** 🕐 Sun.–Thu. 11am–10pm; Fri., Sat. 11am–midnight (bars and restaurants until 3am) 🍽 🎭 🍸 📷 ♿

A small Mediterranean-style village, housing thirty-eight specialty shops, restaurants, cafés, clubs and a large movie theater, CocoWalk is a pleasant open-air meeting place. You can do your shopping, or just window shop, to the rhythm of live music while enjoying the sideshows. **Café Med** has its small tables outside, next door to **Victoria's Secret** (☎ 305/443-2365) with its windows full of lingerie. Nearby are **Banana Republic** (☎ 305/442-6768) and The **White House** (☎ 305/446-7747) selling household linens. The shopping mall gets into full swing in the evenings, when it is like the Venice carnival.

The Streets of Mayfair (42)
2911 Grand Ave, Coconut Grove, FL 33133
☎ (305) 448-1700 ➥ (305) 448-1641

🚌 Bus 6, 22, 27, 42, 48 🅿 charges **Shopping mall** 🕐 Mon. 10am–8pm; Tue.–Sat. 10am–7pm; Sun. noon–5pm 🍽 🎭 🍸 📷 ♿

The diversity of architectural styles matches the diversity in the shops. You can stock up on healthy goods at **Oak Feed Market and Restaurant** (☎ 305/448-7595), a cross between a supermarket and novelty shop also selling vitamins, homeopathic medicines and other New-Age products. On display in **Out of Africa** (☎ 305/445-5900) are beautifully made wooden items from Africa. For men, there is The **French Bazaar** (☎ 305/444-4051), which stocks simple, but colorful hats. If you are after pretty jewelry, try **L.A. Cano** (☎ 305/446-4447) for pre-Colombian-style gold plate items. Not to mention the restaurants, movie theater, ice-cream parlors.

Ritchie Swimwear (43)
3401 Main Hwy, Coconut Grove, FL 33133
☎ (305) 443-7919 ➥ (305) 443-7919

🚌 Bus 6, 22, 27, 42, 48 🅿 charges **Swimwear** 🕐 Mon.–Sat. 10am–9pm; Sun. 11am–7pm 🍽 🏷 800 Ocean Dr, Miami Beach, FL 33133 ☎ (305) 538-0201; Bayside Marketplace ☎ (305) 374-2692

Ritchie designs highly original swimwear for men, women and children. Vital in a town where swimwear is a way of life, not just a sign of the summer. Innovative colors and patterns, fabrics chosen for comfort and elegance. There is no doubt that this is your chance to buy the bathing suit of your dreams!

Not forgetting
■ **Old Navy (44)** 2982 Grand Ave, Coconut Grove, FL 33133 ☎ (305) 448-2227 Casual wear for all, American-style accessories.

41

CocoWalk

41

44

00

42

The construction of CocoWalk, designed to look like a Mediterranean village, has been a huge factor in Coconut Grove's renaissance.

41

42

Toll roads
Miami has several highways with tolls, including the Airport Expressway, which links the airport to the city center, and the East-West Expressway, which links the city center to the Palmetto Expressway.

Getting around

Addresses
If you ask for directions, you will usually be given the nearest cross street, e.g. 700 Ocean Drive at 7th Street.

Distances from Miami to

Daytona Beach: 251 miles/402 km
Fort Lauderdale: 22 miles/35 km
Fort Myers: 141 miles/226 km

Key West: 155 miles/249 km
Orlando: 228 miles/365 km
Tampa: 245 miles/392 km
W. Palm Beach: 64 miles/102 km

6
Maps

In brief

In the United States, names of roads, streets etc. and also directions are often abbreviated. Here are the most common:

Av, Ave: Avenue
Blvd: Boulevard
Cswy: Causeway
Ct: Court
Dr: Drive
E: East

Expwy: Expressway
Hwy: Highway
Ln: Lane
N: North
Pl: Place
Plz: Plaza
Rd: Road
S: South
St: Street
W: West

Ojus
BACARDI BUILDING
N. MIAMI B.
SPANISH MON. CLOISTERS
N. MIAMI
MOCA
MIAMI
The Everglades
HIALEAH
SURFSIDE
AMERICAN POLICE HALL OF FAME AND MUSEUM
A
MIAMI BEACH
MIAMI SPRS.
MIAMI INT. AIRPORT ✈
C
B
SWEETWATER
MIAMI
ATLANTIC OCEAN
W. MIAMI
CORAL GABLES
D
E
Kendall
S. MIAMI
MIAMI SEAQUARIUM
Key Biscayne
PARROT JUNGLE
KENDALL-TAMIAMI AIRPORT ✈
Richmond Hts.

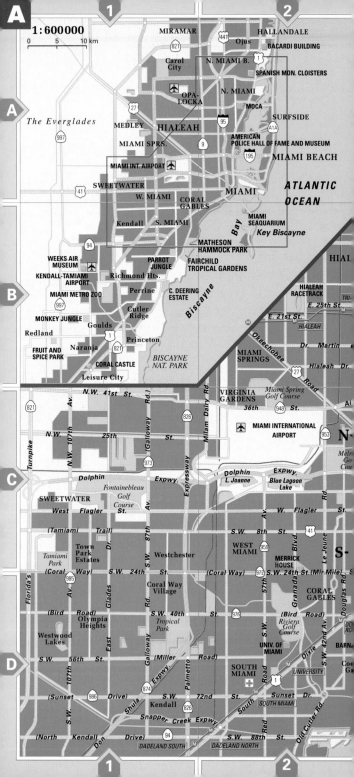

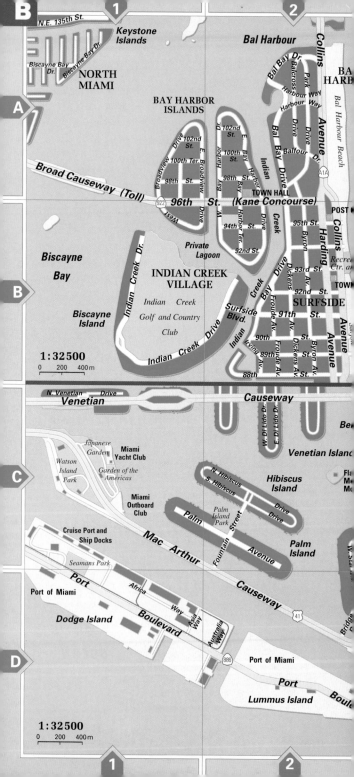

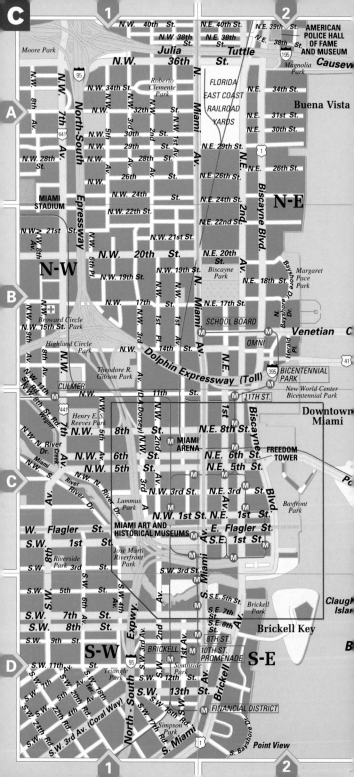

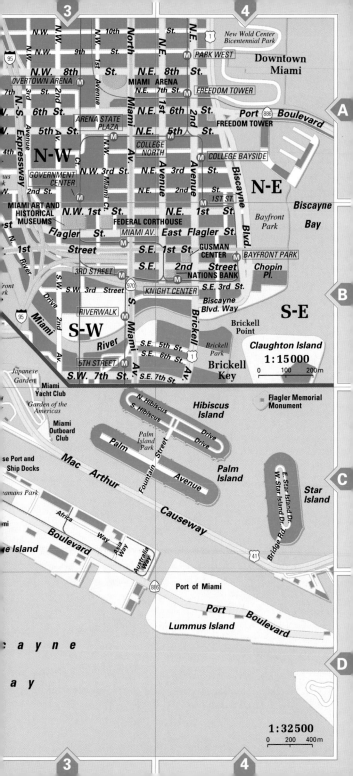

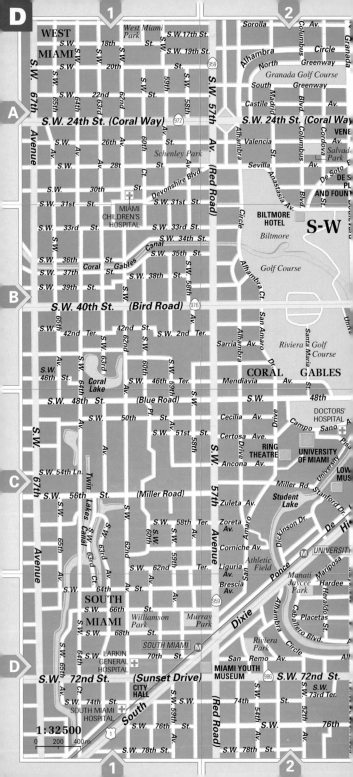

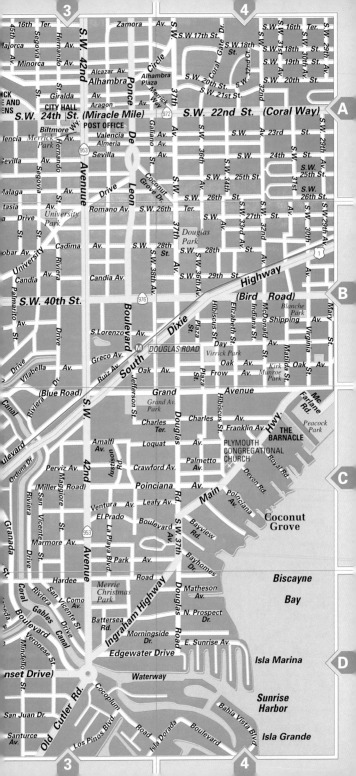

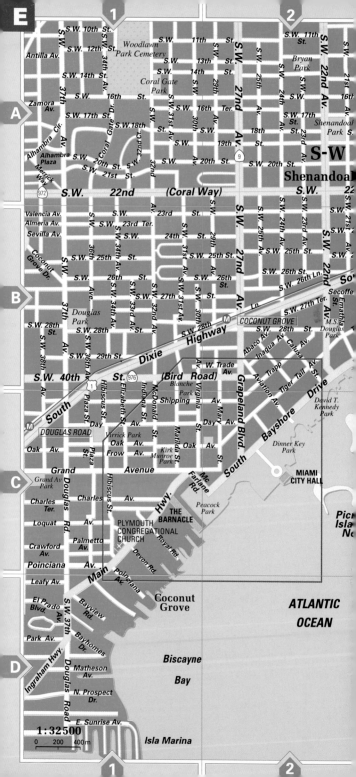

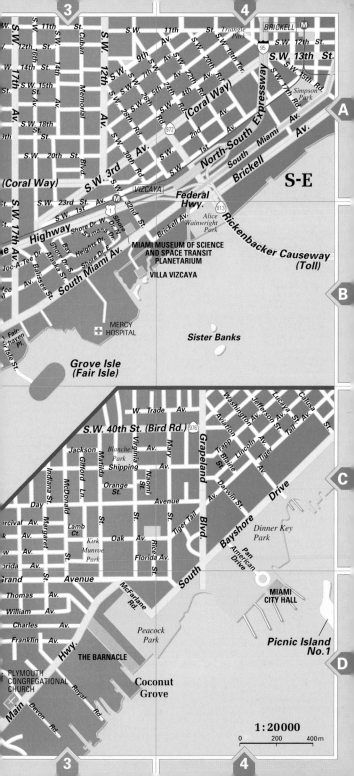

For each street, the letter in bold refers to one of the maps (**A–F**), and the letters and numbers mark the corresponding square in which it is found.

Street
index

A

Abaco Avenue **E** B 2
Adams Avenue North **B** A 4
Africa Way **C** C 3
Airport Expressway **A** C 2-3
Alaska Street **E** B 3
Alcazar Avenue **D** A 3
Alfonso Avenue **D** D 2-3
Alhambra Circle **D** A-B 2-3
Alhambra Circle, South **D** D 2-3
Alhambra Court **D** B 2
Alhambra Drive **D** B-C 2
Alhambra Plaza **D** A 3-4
Alice Wainwright Park **E** B 4
'Allapattah (Metro Station) **A** C 3
Almeria Avenue **D** A 3-4
Altara Avenue **D** B 3
Alton Road **B** A-D 3
Amalfi Avenue **D** C 3
American Police Hall of Fame and Museum **C** A 2
Anastasia Avenue **D** A-B 2-3
Ancona Avenue **D** C 2
Anderson Road **D** A-B 3
Antilla Avenue **E** A 1
Aragon Avenue **D** A 3
Arena State Plaza (Metro Station) **C** A 3
Arthur Godfrey Road **B** A 3-4
Asia Way **C** C 3
Athletic Field **D** C 2
Augusto Street **D** C 2-3
Australia Way **C** C 3
Aviation Avenue **E** C 4

B

Bacardi Building **A** A 2
Bahia Vista Boulevard **D** D 4
Bal Bay Drive **B** A 2
Bal Harbour **B** A 2
Bal Harbour Beach **B** A 2
Balcross Drive **B** A 2
Balfour Drive **B** A 2
Balissee Street **E** B 3
Battersea Road **D** D 3
Bay Drive **B** B 2
Bay Harbor Drive, East **B** A-B 2
Bay Harbor Drive, West **B** A-B 2
Bay Harbor Islands **B** A 1-2
Bay Harbor Terrace **B** A-B 2
Bayberry Drive **E** B 3
Bayfront Park **C** B 4
Bayfront Park (Metro Station) **C** B 4
Bay Point **A** B 3-4
Bayshore Drive, North **C** B 2
Bayshore Drive, South **C** D 2
Bayshore Municipal Golf Course **B** B 3
Baytomes Drive **E** D 1
Bayview Road **E** D 1
Belle Isle **B** C 2
Bicentennial Park (Metro Station) **C** B 2
Bilmore Golf Course **D** B 2
Bilmore Hotel **D** B 2
Biltmore Drive **D** C 3
Biltmore Way **D** A 3
Biscayne Bay **C** A 3-4
Biscayne Bay Drive **B** A 1
Biscayne Boulevard **C** A-B 4
Biscayne Boulevard Way **C** B 4
Biscayne Canal **A** A 3
Biscayne Gardens **A** A 3
Biscayne National Park **A** B 1

Biscayne Park **C** B 2
Biscayne Street **B** D 3-4
Biscayne Waterway **B** A 4
Blaine Street **E** C 4
Blanche Park **E** C 3
Blue Lagoon Lake **A** C 1
Brescia Avenue **D** D 2
Brickell (Metro Station) **C** D 1
Brickell Avenue **C** B 4
Brickell Key **C** B 4
Brickell Park **C** B 4
Bridge Road **C** C 4
Broad Causeway (Toll) **B** A-B 1
Broadview Drive, East **B** A-B 1
Broadview Drive, West **B** A-B 1
Broward Circle Park **C** B 1
Brownsville **A** C 3
Brownsville (Metro Station) **A** B 3
Bryan Park **E** A 2
Buena Vista **C** A 3
Bunche Park **A** A 3
Byron Avenue **B** B 2

C

Caballero Boulevard **D** D 2
Cadima Avenue **D** B 3
Calusa Street **E** C 4
Campo Sano Avenue **D** C 2
Candia Avenue **D** B 3
Cardena Street **D** A-B 3
Carol City **A** A 1
Castaneda Street **D** D 3
Castille Avenue **D** C 3
Cecilia Avenue **D** D 2
Cellini Street **D** D 3
Central Miami Beach **B** A-B 4
Certosa Avenue **D** C 2
Charles Avenue **E** D 3
Charles Deering Estate **A** B 1
Charles Terrace **D** C 3-4
Chase Avenue **B** A 3-4
Chopin Plaza **C** B 4
City Hall (Miami Beach) **B** B-C 3
City Hall (North Miami) **A** A 3
City Hall (Shenandoah) **D** A 3
City Hall (South Miami) **D** D 1
Civic Center (Metro Station) **A** C 3
Claughton Island **C** B 4
Coconut Grove **E** D 3-4
Coconut Grove (Metro Station) **E** B 2
Coconut Grove Drive **D** A-B 3-4
Cocoplum Road **D** D 3
College Bayside (Metro Station) **C** A 4
College North (Metro Station) **C** A 3
Collins Avenue **B** A-B 2
Collins Canal **B** B 3
Collins Park **B** B 4
Columbus Boulevard **D** A 2
Como Avenue **D** D 2
Convention Center Drive **B** B 3
Coral Castle **A** B 1
Coral Gables **D** B 2
Coral Gables Canal **D** B-D 1-3
Coral Gate Drive **E** A 1
Coral Gate Park **E** A 1
Coral Lake **D** B 1
Coral Way **C** D 1
Coral Way Village **A** D 1

Cordova Street **D** A 2•
Corniche Avenue **D** C 2
Crandon Boulevard **A** D 4
Crandon Park **A** D 4
Crawford Avenue **D** C 3-4
Cruise Port and Ship Docks **C** C 3
Cuban Memorial Boulevard **E** A 3
Culmer (Metro Station) **C** C 1
Cutler Ridge **A** B 1

D

Dadeland North (Metro Station) **A** D 2
Dadeland South (Metro Station) **A** D 1
Darwin Street **E** C 4
David T. Kennedy Park **E** C 2
Day Avenue **E** C 3-4
De Soto Boulevard **D** A 2
Devon Road **E** D 3
Devonshire Boulevard **D** A 1
Di Lido Drive, East **B** C 2
Di Lido Drive, West **B** C 2
Dickens Drive **B** B 2
Dickinson Drive **D** C 2
Dinner Key Park **E** C 4
Dixie Highway, South **D** B-D 1-4
Dixie Highway, West **A** A 3-4
Doctors' Hospital **D** C 2
Dodge Island **C** C 3
Dolphin Expressway **C** B 1-2
Donatello Street **D** C 2-3
Don Shula Expressway **A** D 1
Douglas Park **E** B 1
Douglas Road **C** C-D 4
Douglas Road (Metro Station) **E** C 1
Downtown Miami **C** A 4
Dr. Martin Luther King Boulevard **A** B 2-3
Dr. Martin Luther King Junior (Metro Station) **A** B 3
Drexel Avenue **B** C 3
Dumfoundling Bay **A** A 4

E

Earlington Heights (Metro Station) **A** C 3
Edgewater Drive **D** C 3-4
Ed Sullivan Drive **B** A 3
Elizabeth Street **E** B-C 1
El Portal **A** B 3
El Prado Boulevard **D** C 3-4
Emathla Street **E** B 2
Erwin Road (47th Avenue) **D** D 3
Escobar Avenue **D** B 3
Espanola Way **B** C 3-4
Expressway, East-West **A** C 3
Expressway, North-South **C** A-D 1

F

Fairchild Tropical Gardens **A** B 1-2
Fairhaven Place **E** B 3
Fair Isle Street **E** B 3
Federal Courthouse **C** A 3
Federal Highway **E** A-B 4
Financial District (Metro Station) **C** D 2
First Station (Metro Station) **C** A-B 4
Fisher Island **A** C 4
Flagler Memorial Monument **C** C 4
Flagler Street, East **C** B 4
Flagler Street, West **C** B 3
Flamingo Drive **B** A 4
Flamingo Park **B** C 3
Florida Avenue **E** C 3
Florida East Coast Railroad Yards **C** A 2
Florida's Turnpike **A** C-D 1
Fontainebleau Park **A** C 1
Fountain Street **C** C 3-4
Franklin Avenue **E** D 3
Freedom Tower **C** A 4
Freedom Tower (Metro Station) **C** A 4
Froude Avenue **B** B 2
Frow Avenue **E** C 3
Fruit and Spice Park **A** B 1

G

Galiano Street **D** A 3
Garden of the Americas **C** C 3
Gifford Lane **E** C 3
Giralda Avenue **D** A 3
Glades Drive, East **A** C-D 1
Golden Glades **A** A 3
Goulds **A** B 1
Government Center (Metro Station) **C** A 3
Granada Boulevard **D** A-D 2
Granada Golf Course **D** A 2
Grand Avenue **E** D 3
Grand Avenue Park **D** C 3
Grapeland Boulevard **E** C 4
Gratigny Drive **A** A-B 3
Greco Avenue **D** B 3
Greenway Drive, North **D** A 2
Greenway Drive, South **D** A 2
Grove Isle (Fair Isle) **E** B 3
Gusman Center **C** B 4

H

Hallandale **A** A 2
Harbour Way **B** A 2
Hardee Road **D** D 2-3
Harding Avenue **B** A 2
Haulover Beach Park **A** A 4
Henry E. S. Reeves Park **C** C 1
Herald Plaza **C** B 2
Hernando Street **A** A 3
Hialeah **A** B 2
Hialeah (Metro Station) **A** B 2
Hialeah Drive **A** B 2
Hialeah Racetrack **A** B 2
Hibiscus Drive, North **C** C 3-4
Hibiscus Drive, South **C** C 3-4
Hibiscus Island **C** C 4
Hibiscus Street **C** C 4
Highland Circle Park **C** B 1

I

Inagua Street **E** B 2
Indiana Street **E** C 3
Indian Creek **B** A 3
Indian Creek Drive **B** A-B 4
Indian Creek Drive, East **B** B 1-2
Indian Creek Drive, West **B** B 1
Indian Creek Golf and Country Club **B** B 1
Indian Creek Park **B** A 4
Indian Creek Village **B** B 1-2
Ingraham Highway **D** D 3-4
Inlet Boulevard **B** D 3
Irving Avenue **B** B 2
Isla Dorada Boulevard **D** D 3-4
Isla Grande **D** D 4
Isla Marina **E** D 1
Island View Park **B** B 3
Iustison Road **D** C 3

J

Jackie Gleason Theater of the Performing Arts **B** B-C 3-4
Jackson Avenue **E** C 3
Japanese Garden **C** B 3
Jefferson Avenue **B** C 3-4
Jefferson Street **D** B-C 3
Jeronimo Drive **B** B 3
John Fitzgerald Kennedy Causeway **A** B 4
José Martí Riverfront Park **C** B 3
Julia Tuttle Causeway **B** A 3

K

Kendall **A** D 1
Kendall-Tamiami Airport **A** B 1
Key Biscayne **A** D 4
Key Biscayne Village **A** D 4
Keystone Island **B** A 1
Kirk Munroe Park **E** C 3
Knight Center (Metro Station) **C** B 4

L

Lake Joanne **A** C 1
Lake Pancoast **B** B 4

146

33rd Court, South-West
E B 1
33rd Street, South-West
D B 1
34th Avenue, South-West
E A–B 1
34th Street, North-East
C A 2
34th Street, North-West
C A 1
34th Street, South-West
D B 1
34th Street, West **B** A 4
35th Street, West **B** A 4
36th Avenue, South-West
E B 1
36th Street **A** C 2
36th Street, North-West
C A 1-2
36th Street, South-West
D B 1
37th Avenue **E** D 1
37th Avenue, South-West
E A–B 1
37th Street, South-West
D B 1
37th Street, West **B** A 4
38th Avenue, South-West
D B 3-4
38th Street, North-East
C A 2
38th Street, North-West
C A 1-2
38th Street, South-West
D B 1
39th Street, North-East
C A 2
39th Street, South-West
D B 1

40th Street, North-East
C A 1-2
40th Street (Bird Road),
South-West **D** B 1-4
40th Street, West **B** A 4
41st Street, North-West
A C 1
41st Street, West **B** A 4
42nd Avenue, South-West
D A–D 3
42nd Street **D** B 1
42nd Terrace, South-West
D B 1-2
43rd Street, West **B** A 4
44th Court, West
B A 3-4
44th Street, West **B** A 4
45th Avenue **D** A 3
46th Street, South-West
D B 1
46th Street, West **B** A 4
48th Street (Blue Road),
South-West **D** C 1
50th Street, South-West
D C 1
51st Street, South-West
D C 1-2
52th Avenue, South-West
D D 2
54th Avenue, South-West
D D 2
54th Lincoln, South-West
D C 1
54th Street, North-West
A B 3
56th Street (Miller Road),
South-West **D** C 1
57th Avenue (Red Road),
South-West **D** A–D 2

58th Avenue, South-West
D A–D 1
58th Terrace, South-West
D C 1-2
59th Avenue, South-West
D A–D 1
60th Avenue, South-West
D C–D 1
60th Court, South-West
D A 1
60th Place, South-West
D B–C 1
62nd Avenue, South-West
D A–D 1
62nd Terrace, South-West
D C 1-2
63rd Avenue, South-West
D A–D 1
63rd Court, South-West
D C–D 1
64th Avenue, South-West
D A–D 1
64th Street, South-West
D D 1
65th Avenue, South-West
D A–D 1
66th Street, South-West
D D 1
67th Avenue **D** A–D 1
68th Street, South-West
D D 1
70th Street, South-West
D D 1
72nd Street (Sunset Drive),
South-West **D** D 1-3
73rd Terrace, South-West
D D 2
74th Street, South-West
D D 1-2

76th Street, South-West
D D 1-2
78th Street, South-West
D D 1-2
79th Street, North-West
A B 3
87th Avenue (Galloway
Road), South-West
A C–D 1
88th Street (North Kendall
Drive) **A** D 1-2
89th Street **B** B 2
90th Street **B** B 2
91th Street **B** B 2
92nd Street **B** B 2
93rd Street **B** B 2
94th Street **B** B 2
95th Street **B** B 2
95th Street, North-West
A B 3
96th Street
(Kane Concourse)
B A–B 1-2
98th Street **B** A 1-2
100th Street **B** A 2
100th Terrace **B** A 1
102nd Street **B** A 1-2
103rd Street, North-West
A B 3
107th Avenue, North-West
A C 1
107th Avenue, South-West
A D 1
125th Street, North-East
A A 3-4
135th Street, North-East
A A 3-4
135th Street, North-West
A A 3

Subway map

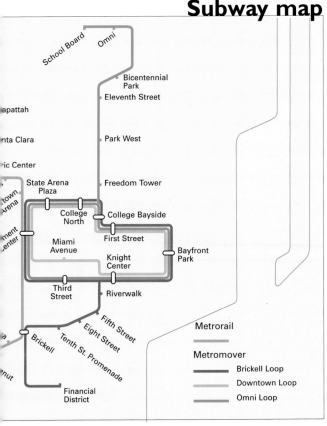

School Board
Omni
Bicentennial Park
Eleventh Street
apattah
nta Clara
ic Center
Park West
Freedom Tower
State Arena Plaza
College North
College Bayside
First Street
Miami Avenue
Knight Center
Bayfront Park
Third Street
Riverwalk
Fifth Street
Eight Street
Tenth St. Promenade
Brickell
Financial District

Metrorail

Metromover
Brickell Loop
Downtown Loop
Omni Loop

For practical and other information, as well as useful contact numbers concerning travel and life in Miami, see the 'Getting there' section on pages 6 to 13.

General

index

The publisher would like to thank the City of Miami, the Greater Miami Convention & Visitors Bureau and all who helped in the preparation of this guide.

Picture
Credits